CATECHESIS FOR LITURGY

A PROGRAM FOR PARISH INVOLMEMENT

GILBERT OSTDIEK, OFM

WITH INTRODUCTION BY THOMAS GROOME

PASTORAL PRESS
Portland, Oregon

ISBN 0-912405-23-6

Contents

II
INVOLVING THE PARISH

Introduction
"Catechesis for a New Liturgical Consciousness"

Historians of liturgy tell us that there was a time in the early church when the liturgy was enacted by the action of the whole assembly. Traces of liturgy as communal participative action can still be found into the Middle Ages when Sunday worship amounted to a day-long festival and celebration for the whole community.[1] But for the church in which most of today's adults were raised, and for hundreds of years before our time, the liturgy was a spectator event for the people, something performed for us. Since the people were not consciously aware of their priests as called forth by the whole community, priests were seen more as God's representatives than ours. A feeble symbolic representation of the people could be seen in the altar servers, but that was feeble indeed and required a goodly stretch of the imagination. In other words, liturgy was brought to us as a gift from God rather than arising from among us as a participative event. It was done for us or to us but not by us.

What an extraordinary revolution it was, then, when Vatican II declared that the liturgy is to be the action of the whole People of God in which all the members of the Body of Christ have a right, by baptism, to actively participate. In its *Constitution on the Sacred Liturgy*, the Council declared that "in the liturgy the whole public worship is performed by the Mystical Body of Jesus Christ, that is, by the Head and his members ... it is an action of Christ the Priest and his Body which is the Church" (CSL #7 [DOL #7]). It went on to insist that "the Church earnestly desires that all the faithful be led to that full, conscious, and active participation in

---

1. See Aidan Kavanagh, *On Liturgical Theology* (New York: Pueblo Publishing Co., 1981), especially chap. 4.

liturgical celebrations called for by the very nature of the liturgy. Such participation by the Christian people ... is their right and duty by reason of their baptism" (CSL #14 [DOL #14]). In light of where we had come from, such sentiments were nothing short of an invitation to turn our liturgical world upside down.

But reflect for a moment on the kind of catechesis for liturgy that such "full, conscious and active participation" will require of a people whose primary socialization was into passivity. Quite obviously it demands a transformation in consciousness on the part of both people and ministers, a new awareness of the whole community as the liturgical agent. Such an educational task cannot be fulfilled by some form of what Paulo Freire calls "banking education" (depositing information in passive receptacles) that simply brings people "up to date" on the liturgical changes. It requires, instead, a critical and consciousness-raising pedagogical process that can help to form a new liturgical identity and disposition in our people, an awareness of ourselves as full participants by right and with responsibility for the liturgical action.

In *Catechesis for Liturgy*, Gil Ostdiek makes a most valuable contribution toward promoting such a consciousness-raising liturgical catechesis. He proposes an integrated program of pastoral care for the liturgy consisting of catechesis, preparation, and evaluation. He then uses those categories to review the themes of space, time, action and speech, what he calls the "languages of liturgy." It is the catechetical process which Ostdiek proposes that holds his most promising and revolutionary contribution.

I might well be suspected of some bias here, since the process he proposes is an adapted form of the shared praxis approach with which my own work is closely identified. But Ostdiek's adaptation of the five movements of shared praxis into attending, reflecting (which includes the community Story and Vision), and applying is most creative. It promises to be a compelling way to engage people, not simply to learn *about* liturgy, but to develop a liturgical consciousness and identity that promotes their active and full participation.

I earnestly hope that this book will not merely be read but used widely, because it is the actual operationalizing of such catechesis for liturgy that will help to incarnationalize the liturgical revolution to which the Church has called us. I am confident that the parishes and communities which use Ostdiek's approach will experience an amazing renewal in their liturgical actions and in the faith life of their people. Only by some such process will liturgy become in reality, and not merely in theory, "the summit toward which the activity of the Church is directed; ... the fount from which all the Church's power flows" (CSL #10 [DOL #10]).

Thomas H. Groome
Associate Professor of
Theology and Religious
  Education
Boston College

Abbreviations

CSL   *Constitution on the Sacred Liturgy (Sacrosanctum Concilium)*, decreed by Vatican Council II, Dec. 4, 1963

DOL   *Documents on the Liturgy, 1963-1979. Conciliar, Papal, and Curial Texts*, collected and translated by the International Commission on English in the Liturgy (Collegeville: Liturgical Press, 1982)

EACW   *Environment and Art in Catholic Worship*, issued by the NCCB Bishops' Committee on the Liturgy (Washington, D.C.: USCC, 1978)

GIRM   *General Instruction of the Roman Missal*, issued by the Sacred Congregation for Divine Worship in 1975

GNLYC   *General Norms for the Liturgical Year and the Calendar*, issued by the Sacred Congregation of Rites in 1969

ILM   *Introduction to the Lectionary for the Mass*, issued in 1969 and revised in 1981 by the Sacred Congregation for the Sacraments and Divine Worship, translated by the International Commission on English in the Liturgy (Washington, D.C.: USCC, 1982)

LMT   *Liturgical Music Today*, issued by the NCCB Bishops' Committee on the Liturgy (Washington, D.C: USCC, 1982)

MCW   *Music in Catholic Worship*, issued by the NCCB Bishops' Committee on the Liturgy in 1972 and revised in 1983 (Washington, D.C.: USCC, 1983)

Preface

This volume is addressed to those who are charged with the pastoral care of God's people at prayer: catechists, planners, and ministers of the liturgy.

This book is not intended as a pastoral aid in the usual sense of the word. Since Vatican II many valuable pastoral aids have been published to give liturgical catechists, planners, and ministers the immediate help we need in preparing the rites, the people we serve, and ourselves for the celebration of the revised liturgy. Those aids are more than adequate for the task.

A number of convictions persuade me to take a different approach in what is written here. The new liturgy has taken root in our lives and is producing a healthy sense of what it means to be a local community gathered at prayer. That experience also bears within it the seeds of a broader understanding of what it means to care for God's people at prayer. It challenges us to be attentive to the ways in which the liturgy speaks to each assembly and to develop an integrated approach to catechesis, preparation, and celebration of the liturgy which is responsive to the assembly's experience.

This book, then, is an invitation to look beyond the immediate, technical demands we face in teaching, preparing, and celebrating the liturgy. It is an invitation to reflect more fully on our experience of the past two decades and to learn its lessons. It is an invitation to think in larger ways about the liturgical ministry we share and to see catechesis as the vital first step in that ministry. But it is only an invitation. There is no ready-made program of pastoral care that will serve us all; we each need to shape a program suited to the needs and resources of our people. This book will have served its purpose if that invitation is heard. My fondest dreams will have come true if readers make the ideas their own and set the book aside.

I owe a debt of gratitude to many who have helped shape the contents of this book and bring it into being. Participants and students in countless parish workshops and courses on liturgy have by their response encouraged me to develop the materials and methods presented here. I have gained inspiration and freely borrowed insights from my colleagues in the North American Academy of Liturgy's study group working on the ritual dimension of liturgy. Thomas Groome, who so graciously agreed to introduce these pages, has provided both theory and method to undergird my efforts. I would never have begun to write the book without the insistent invitation of Virgil Funk, president of the National Association of Pastoral Musicians and its Pastoral Press, and I would never have finished it without the patient care he and editor Dan Connors exercised to the end. Catholic Theological Union granted me a sabbatical season to do the writing, and the friars of the Old Mission in Santa Barbara, California, welcomed me with warm hospitality into their special place of quiet peace while I wrote. Several friends and colleagues in the work of pastoral liturgy were also of great help to me: Kathleen Hughes, R.S.C.J., Mary Catherine Keane, S.P., and Kathleen Sullivan-Stewart critiqued parts of the manuscript for me; Gabe Huck wrote a word of recommendation. To each of them, my heartfelt thanks!

Finally, I wish to say a special word of thanks to my family and friends who have helped me learn the ways liturgy speaks to us and who have been a constant support as I have tried to capture something of those ways on these pages. To them I gratefully dedicate this book.

> Gilbert Ostdiek, O.F.M.
> Word and Worship Department
> Catholic Theological Union

I
THE PROGRAM

Introduction

A word about the book's perspective

It is only right that I begin by naming some important assumptions that lie behind this book.

Liturgy is not a thing. It is the act of a people who gather with the Risen Lord to keep covenant with God - to hear God's word, to pray, to offer thanks and praise for the marvelous thing God has done for us in Jesus, and to leave with a mission. It is a moment in which we lift up the outward deeds and inner movements of our daily lives to allow them to be enlightened with a Gospel word and to be signed with a gesture of dying and rising. Liturgy is a verb, filled with a people's celebrating and living.

Catechesis for liturgy is not catechetical text or technique. It, too, is an action. It is the act of God's people who gather to reflect together on the liturgy we celebrate. But such catechesis is not just *about* liturgy, it is also *for* the liturgy. In reflecting together on the liturgy, we seek to name and deepen the meaning that holy moment has for us, both when we are gathered and when we are out on mission in our world living as God's pilgrim people. Liturgical catechesis is a verb, filled with a people's shared reflecting for the sake of liturgy and life.

These ways of seeing liturgy and catechesis in turn suggest a number of perspectives and concerns which ought to frame the contents of this book.

In the first place, our perspective must always focus on the assembly. The liturgy is the event of the assembly, not simply the action of its liturgical ministers. Catechesis is that assembly's shared reflection on the mystery it celebrates, not simply the input of its catechists. Our pastoral care must center not on our roles of service, on what to do and how to do it, but on the people's action.

Even as we talk about our roles of service in this book, we will try to keep our focus on the assembly, rather than ourselves. But that is not always easy for people trained in the art of pastoral care and dedicated to its exercise. Our subtle temptation is to see pastoral care as a unilateral service we do *for* the people, rather than as a service we perform in their midst, a service marked by mutuality and meant to enable both them and us to name and celebrate the mystery of God's presence in our lives. If we give the assembly pride of place, however, it lends our ministry a deep sense of grounding in and solidarity with the people we serve.

Second, we need to take the assembly's experience of the liturgy as our point of departure and constant reference. To be sure, our rich liturgical heritage and the revised rites of Vatican II mold and shape our experience of the liturgy and what it can mean for us, but heritage and text only take on living meaning for a people in the moment of celebration. The meaning we wish to search out, reflect on, and prepare to enact is not simply that which is contained in a catechism or ritual book, it is the meaning a liturgy actually has for the people who gather to celebrate it. Our pastoral care must center not on a book, but on the people and their experience.

To focus on our experience of the liturgy, as we will constantly do in this book, entails a letting go. One of the occupational hazards we all face in caring for the liturgy is our desire to ensure a meaningful liturgy - using history and text to determine beforehand and unambiguously what that meaning should be for our people. We can afford to take the risk of letting go if we trust that God's Spirit is at work in the people, helping all of us together to attain a deeper understanding of the saving gift given us in the word we receive and in the mysteries we celebrate. And we will discover, to our delight, that we all do have a common covenant story to tell, needing only the words to name it.

Third, we need to cultivate a largeness of vision about our liturgical ministry. We need to move beyond the mechanics of lesson plans and ritual performance to a sense of serving God's people at prayer. We need to understand that catechesis, preparation, and performance of liturgy are so many threads which are to be woven together to form a larger tapestry of liturgical ministry. Our pastoral care for God's people at prayer must center not on the liturgical moment alone, but on the life journeys which the liturgy names and celebrates.

Reaching for a larger vision of liturgical ministry, as we will try to do in this book, may seem to be a luxury. We all face the inexorable, grinding pressures of providing good catechesis and liturgical celebration week after week. Can we afford the time for such dreaming? Perhaps the question needs to be reversed. Can we afford not to, if we are not willing to risk being forced into mindlessly tending the store? Dreams have a way of clarifying what really matters and infusing new life into the drudgery of our daily routine.

These are the perspectives and concerns that shape this book as a whole. An additional preoccupation underlies the second part, namely, our almost exclusive reliance on verbal language as the bearer of meaning in liturgy to the neglect of the other ways in which the liturgy speaks to us. More will be said about that in part two.

A word about this part

This part of the book will sketch a framework for a larger approach to pastoral care for the liturgy. The first chapter will focus on catechesis for liturgy, the vital first step in that approach, and sketch a method that might be used. Chapter two will take up and develop the joint issues of preparing and evaluating the liturgy, which build on catechesis and complete the cycle of caring for the liturgy. Chapter three will wrestle with the question of what qualities to look for in preparing and evaluating liturgical celebrations. Chapter four will set catechesis, preparation, and evaluation within a vision of liturgy and liturgical ministry and propose that they be gathered into a larger, integrated program of pastoral care for God's people at prayer.

1

Catechesis for Liturgy

WE HAVE REACHED A UNIQUE "TEACHABLE MOMENT" IN OUR liturgical life. The signs are all around us. In many parishes and communities liturgical ministers and people alike are hungering more and more for an effective catechesis on the ways and meanings of the new liturgy. To be sure, there was a concerted effort to provide introductory explanations and education programs as each new rite was introduced and as people took up the various liturgical ministries. But we often conducted the programs hastily and under pressure, and we did not yet have enough experience of those rites under our belts to benefit fully from the catechesis given then. The backlog of liturgical experience accumulated since then has left us with new questions and a new need to name and reflect on the meaning of that experience. We are ready for a second, fuller phase of the liturgical instruction called for in Vatican II (CSL #14-20, 35 [DOL #14-20, 35]).

The Council established a clear pastoral goal for our catechesis: people are to receive liturgical instruction enabling them to participate fully in the liturgy in keeping with their way of life and spiritual development (CSL #19 [DOL #19]).[1] That will not happen unless a program of liturgical formation enables pastors and liturgical ministers themselves to "become thoroughly imbued with the spirit and power of the liturgy and make themselves its teachers" (CSL #14 [DOL #14]).

But how are we to go about that educational task? There is no ready-made answer to that question. Neither Vatican II nor our recent tradition of liturgical catechesis offered us any concrete program or design suited to our needs, and each community has been left to seek out its own. This chapter will offer some reflections and suggestions that may help in that search.[2]

CATECHESIS FOR LITURGY

The first thing to do is to sort out what we mean by liturgical catechesis.

When we hear the word 'catechesis' we normally associate it with the catechism classes we attended as youngsters. The classes may have been taught in a CCD or religious education program or in a Catholic school as part of our daily schedule of courses. As in other forms of education, there were pupils and a teacher. There was also a fixed set of material to be learned, usually available for our "homework" in the form of a text or catechism. In the course of several years we covered all the major areas of Catholic belief and moral practice, and there was special preparation for the first reception of sacraments.

By engaging in this bit of nostalgic reminiscing, however, we may be unwittingly limiting our view of catechesis to what goes on in a classroom. The root meaning of the word itself, "oral instruction," can be much broader. The classroom model, with its written text and fixed fund of information to be imparted, is not the only way in which education happens. As adults we constantly learn from our experience by reflecting on it, often with the help of someone who is experienced and wise. We ought not presume from the beginning, then, that liturgical catechesis must be a form of classroom learning. Later on in this chapter we will explore an alternate model.

There is a second limitation which we should also eliminate from the very start. Liturgical catechesis is not necessarily the same as the sacramental catechesis we received before first reception of the sacraments. In the past sacramental catechesis has tended to focus more on the inner, theological meaning of the sacrament than on the experience of the rite itself. It also focused too exclusively on the sacramental moments, rather than on the liturgy as a whole. That kind of sacramental catechesis is too narrow a model for our purposes.

What, then, is liturgical catechesis? Liturgical catechesis takes two forms that are each important and significantly different from the other.

The first can be called *catechesis through liturgy*. The liturgy itself is a form of catechesis. We learn how to do the liturgy through repeated participation in it. More importantly, and on a deeper level, the readings, prayers, and gestures work together over long periods of time to shape our ways of perceiving and living out our lives. Attitudes, values, and ways of acting are subtly nurtured through the liturgy.[3] Without a doubt the liturgy has a formative power. It is a catechesis in its own right.

But a caution is necessary at this point. The primary focus of such catechesis through liturgy is not on the liturgy itself, but on christian living. Liturgy is not meant to be a classroom session and it suffers greatly when it is turned into a preachy, didactic affair or when it turns in on itself and becomes excessively occupied with explaining itself.

The qualities that ensure a liturgy's healthy catechetical impact are not hard to identify. Three seem especially critical. The first is that the liturgical actions, words, and symbols have an obvious integrity and authenticity about them and an ability to speak to the experience of the people assembled. The second is the sense of care and reverence with which words are spoken, actions performed, and symbolic objects produced and presented. The third is the sense of personal presence at prayer manifested by the assembly and especially by its liturgical ministers. This last is perhaps the most critical of all. Without prayer even the most relevant and beautifully crafted liturgical performance remains only an empty shell.

Together, qualities such as these ensure that we experience the actions of the liturgy as something more than their everyday, non-liturgical counterparts. Liturgical action is experienced as sacrament, an outward sign of a holy reality beyond itself, when we are instinctively led by its manner of being done to ask the question of the youngest child at the Jewish Seder, "Why is this night different from all other nights?" Effective liturgy hinges on such seemingly small things as a welcome that is sincere, a prayer that is meant, a reverent bow that is more than a casual bobbing of the head, and bread that can bear the burden of signing shared life. In the end it depends most of all on assembled people and ministers whose faith and prayer are apparent and contagious. Catechesis through liturgy is assured in such liturgical celebrations. It cannot help but happen.

Catechesis through liturgy is the most important form of liturgical catechesis. Its goal is the deepening of christian living, and it touches both the assembly and its ministers. To provide for the kind of "cared for" liturgy envisioned here a second, auxiliary kind of catechesis is needed, both for the assembly as a whole and for those who function as the liturgical ministers of the assembly.

This second form of liturgical catechesis can be called *catechesis for liturgy*. As the phrase suggests, the goal of this form of liturgical catechesis is to prepare people to participate in the liturgy. We normally do this catechesis in advance of the celebration, though the revised rites do make provision for brief catechesis of this kind during the actual celebration.

Let me draw out several contrasts. Unlike catechesis through liturgy, this second form of catechesis focuses deliberately and directly on the liturgy itself. But it is not just rehearsal or training in how to do the liturgy, nor is it a form of theological reflection done in abstraction from the actual celebration, like sacramental catechesis of the past. Rather, it is a reflection on the liturgical rites which seeks to break them open to the understanding of the participants.

This form of liturgical catechesis is of particular importance for liturgical ministers if they are to perform their leadership roles effectively. For if those who are the single most critical factor in enabling a celebration to nourish the assembly's faith (MCW #5-6, 10, 21) are not well formed in and attentive to the ways in which the liturgy speaks, they will not be effective models for and servants of the assembly's prayer. Such catechesis must be extended beyond the liturgical ministers, however. If all God's people have a baptismal right to participate in the liturgy with full understanding and spiritual benefit, then this second kind of catechesis is also theirs by right. Leaving it to chance, or to the example of the liturgical ministers, hardly respects their rights.

Catechesis for the liturgy will be our concern for the remainder of this book, and whenever the phrase 'liturgical catechesis' occurs hereafter, it refers to this form. It is for this catechesis that we will now try to search out a design.

INITIAL ASSUMPTIONS AND PRINCIPLES

Before we sketch such an actual design, it is important to take a look at some initial assumptions and principles that will be crucial for how we decide to carry out liturgical catechesis. Three sets of such assumptions and principles, derived from both liturgy and pedagogy, deserve our attention.

First, the typical christian community includes members who span all stages of life and christian growth, from infants to old timers, from beginning believers to the seasoned and mature. At times small segments of the community gather for special group liturgies, for example, liturgies for children, for youth, for catechumens, for the elderly who seek anointing, and so on. We instinctively understand, however, that those who attend special group liturgies will rejoin the larger liturgical assembly, that the young will eventually attend with and as adults. And the typical liturgical assembly includes members from every stage of growth and development. Adult, mature participation in liturgy is the goal and norm of all celebration.

This suggests several things about liturgical instruction. Worshipers in every phase of life have need of it, not just children and beginners. It has to be available at every stage of growth in forms attuned to each stage. As the worshipers pass through these stages, liturgical instruction must accompany them. It should be gradual and developmental, not segmented and sporadic. Adult, mature participation in the liturgy should be the goal and norm of all liturgical catechesis. Since we often worship together in mixed groups, some form of simultaneous catechesis would also seem to be in place. This suggests that methods and styles of adult education will provide the normative model for liturgical catechesis.

Second, in keeping with the Vatican II mandate that the liturgy be celebrated by an assembly of people who participate fully, actively, and consciously (CSL #14, 27 [DOL #14, 27]), the liturgy has once again become the shared action of a community of believers.

Several helpful ideas for liturgical catechesis flow from this. Taking its cue from adult education, liturgical catechesis will aim to help worshipers learn from their own experience. That experience, rather than pre-established theoretical content, will provide the material. The most apt pedagogical model would be some form of reflection on action, as opposed to the more abstract, theoretical forms of learning we normally associate with the classroom. Ideally the reflection should be done together rather than alone, since the action itself is shared by a community of believers. And the focus of the reflection will naturally go beyond the mechanics of the liturgical action to its meaning for the believers.

Third, the meaning that the liturgical experience has for us is not primarily mental. Liturgy is an action, something to be done. It is the embodying, in human speech and gesture, of God's word and deed for us and of our response to that word and deed. Effective liturgy evokes and enacts the relationship between God and us. To the extent that it is effective, every liturgical action, including speech, enables us to experience the meaning of our lives as God's people. Liturgy is a matter of experienced meaning, not of explanations. In liturgy we say and do what is meaningful; we do not just talk about it. The meaning is embedded in the action; it is an enacted meaning.

Let me take this one step further. The actions of the liturgy, whether speech or gesture, are symbolic actions. That is, the words we hear and the actions we perform embody in sensory form that inner, marvelous exchange between God and ourselves. Or to use a familiar traditional term, liturgical action is by its very nature sacramental in the deepest sense of that word. It is an outward sign which expresses and conveys a hidden, graced reality. The meaning liturgy has for us is enacted symbolically.

This symbolic character of the liturgical action deserves a little further attention here. I would like to highlight three aspects that have been developed in studies on symbol and symbolic action.

These studies have shown that symbols and symbolic actions are capable of bearing a wealth and variety of meaning at one and the same time. Take, for example, our experience of lighting a candle to dispel darkness. This simple experience carries with it the memory imprint of all the times we have experienced both darkness and light. It evokes, without our noticing it, our accumulated feelings of those experiences and of our experience of what it means to come out of the dark into the light. And as we live through this kind of experience with others and explore its meaning with them, we discover that there is both a kinship and a personal uniqueness in what the experience means for each of us. Like any symbolic action, liturgy is filled with a wealth and variety of meanings. These meanings may not only differ but even conflict with one another. They inevitably defy any easy logical "explanation."

These studies have also noted that symbol and symbolic action appeal to the whole person, not just the mind. The meaning they evoke is emotionally charged. To return to the example of lighting the candle, notice how we name the meaning of darkness and light in terms of our feelings - a sense of aloneness or togetherness, of fear or comfort. The meaning the liturgy conveys symbolically is a felt meaning.

Finally, these studies have discovered that symbolic interaction is the form of communication we most rely on in relating with one another. We constantly build, maintain, and repair our relationships through a whole variety of symbols and symbolic actions like touching, shaking hands, sharing food, and hugging one another. Actions such as these go far beyond a mere passing on of information; in them we share ourselves. They go beyond being actions done for purely pragmatic material ends; through them we bond ourselves to one another. This happens in part because shared symbolic action evokes in each of us not only our own unique experience, as in the case of the candle lighting above, but also the discovery that that experience is in some way common to each of us. In similar fashion, the meaning enacted in liturgical symbols centers on relationships.

The fact that liturgy symbolically enacts meaning has important implications for liturgical catechesis. In liturgy we know our God as present and ourselves as graced disciples by the very doing of the action. That "knowing" is less a matter of "knowing about" than it is a shared, felt sense of meaning. Liturgical catechesis should therefore be a process which helps us name and deepen that awareness of being God's people. It is not meant to impart a fixed content or pre-determined block of information, but to heighten and deepen our awareness of our individual and collective relationship to our God and to each other. In carrying out this task liturgical catechesis will take the symbolic actions we do together in liturgy as its starting point and constantly seek to discover the experience they evoke in us, the rich and varied meanings they have for us as God's people.

OUTLINES OF A METHOD

How, then, are we to go about instructing ourselves and others for full, adult participation in the liturgy?

If what we have said above, about how symbolic actions evoke experience and convey meaning, is true, then we ought not look for one iron-clad, detailed design that we can apply to our individual situations literally and without any further ado. There is no one such method at hand. What we can realistically hope to do is sketch in general strokes the rough outline of a method consistent with what we have said and leave it to each of us to develop it, alter it, and flesh it out fully for our real-life situations. My intent here is to offer no more than such a sketch.

In addition to my own experience in adult education workshops in liturgy, two models developed by others have had a great impact on the method I will sketch below.

The first model is an ancient one, developed by the church some fifteen hundred years ago. It is called "mystagogical catechesis" and took place as the final stage of the initiation of adults into the church.

Prior to their actual sacramental initiation during the Easter Vigil, the prospective converts had gone through a prolonged period of formation in christian living and faith. This period, which normally lasted a year or more, was called the catechumenate. During it the catechumens were simply apprentices sharing christian life in all its phases: prayer, service for others, and all that makes up the life of the community. In addition to learning the christian way of living, they received instruction in christian beliefs, but little about the sacraments themselves. When they had matured in the christian way of living and believing, they were chosen to go on to sacramental initiation and spent the lenten season preparing for that great moment.

During the Easter Vigil the chosen catechumens were baptized, confirmed, and admitted to the eucharistic table for the first time. The candidates could not have helped but approach these sacramental rites with a heightened sense of suspense. The long months of waiting and expectation had peaked with several days of fasting, prayer, and the immediate preparations. The rites to be undergone were an unknown mystery to them; they had had only the barest explanations, if any, of what was about to happen. We can imagine what a powerful impact these rites must have had on them, what a sense of awe must have overtaken them as the rites unfolded. They gathered in the midst of a darkness broken only by flickering candle-light, facing first the darkness as they renounced Satan, and then the light as they promised to adhere to Christ. Wave after wave of new experience washed over them as they were unclothed and immersed in the water, anointed with fragrant oil from head to foot, clothed in fresh white robes and jubilantly brought in torchlight procession for the first time into the midst of the assembly gathered for eucharist. The meaning of that momentous event was left for them to experience first; it was not explained beforehand. There was time enough for that later on.

The period after Easter was spent reveling in what had happened, in reflecting on its meaning. It was called the time of "mystagogy," or "mystagogical catechesis," because the newly baptized continued to gather weekly with the bishop to reflect on the meaning of the "mysteries" they had lived through. In those gatherings the bishop helped them relive, detail by detail, the rites they had experienced and he instructed them on the meaning of those rites.

There are several lessons to be learned from this ancient model of liturgical catechesis. The actual experience of the liturgical rites is the starting point and central focus for catechesis of the liturgy. Those rites can be celebrated effectively without an extensive catechesis beforehand. In fact, our catechesis for sacramental celebrations might gain a vividness and freshness if we, like the early church, were to risk delaying it until after the reception of a sacrament. That ancient approach was not without its wisdom; it is hard to talk about something you haven't experienced. This would mean that our preparation for first sacraments would have to take on a different character, perhaps along the lines of a spiritual retreat. Its main goal would be to heighten the recipients' awareness of God's presence and call in their lives, to help them open themselves to God's saving touch, to be experienced in a fresh, heightened way in the sacramental moment. Extended catechesis would then follow the celebration.

The catechumenate process described above has been restored in our church as a result of Vatican II. The model of liturgical catechesis enshrined there is being recovered in a variety of ways in many good catechumenate programs across the country. I have chosen to present the ancient version here because of the clear and consistent way it is recorded in many of the patristic writers and because it represents a rich inheritance from our ancient tradition.

The second model from which I have drawn is a contemporary one, developed by Thomas Groome on the basis of both his pastoral experience and his doctoral studies in religious education for adults. He calls his method "shared christian praxis."[4]

In Groome's mind there are a number of critical assumptions behind the educational process. People before us have learned from their experience, and one of education's tasks is to preserve and hand on that wisdom for the sake of those who will come after. But we, too, learn from our experience. The tradition we receive is not simply some inert deposit of knowledge. So it is also education's task to allow what we have learned from our own experience to enter into true dialogue with that tradition and to reconstruct it and give it new life in our context. Thus our stories and the story we learn from the past flow together to form the living stream of tradition. And the whole point of handing on this shared wisdom is to shape and care for the future. That is education's final task, to make it possible for the vision of the future, enshrined in that living stream of wisdom flowing out of the past, to find new life, to be envisioned anew in our dreams for the future. Thus our visions and the vision we learn from the past merge into one wellspring for the future.

This understanding has led Groome to design a five-step approach to religious education. The first two steps are learner-oriented activities, in which the learners name and share their own experience and the stories and visions it embodies. The third step is one of input, in which the larger community's story and vision are told. The final two steps, again learner-centered, consist of the internal dialogue between those two sets of stories and visions, and provide for decision and follow-up action by the learners.

What can we learn from Groome's method? It names for us what all good educators know in their bones, that we learn best from our own experience, by comparing the unknown with what we already know. Groome offers an easy, adaptable methodology for working with adult learners.[5] And best of all, those who use the method quickly learn that christians reflecting on their own experience discover there, in their own language, what theology can only name in ways that are much more abstract and removed from daily experience. For these and other reasons I have found it extremely valuable in my own work in liturgical catechesis.

With these two models in mind, let us now sketch the outlines of a method for carrying out the pastoral task of liturgical catechesis.

The goal of the method is to enable liturgy planners and committees on the local level to do their own liturgical catechesis for themselves and the communities they serve. It requires only worshipers who are willing to talk about their experience of liturgy and a leader or resource person who can listen to them, draw them out, and help them set their experience in fruitful dialogue with the larger experience of the christian community.

The method has three steps:

1. **attending** to what we and others actually experience at liturgy;
2. **reflecting** on what our experience and that of others means;
3. **applying** what we have learned to future celebration of the liturgy.

Let me describe each of these steps briefly. They will be illustrated more fully in the chapters of part two of this book.

Attending. In the first step we ask ourselves what we experience at liturgy. We can only learn from our liturgical experience if we attend to it and become aware of it. Attending to our experience of liturgy involves recovering it, describing it, and naming it.

When we are caught up in doing something, whether that be our daily work, leisure activity, or interacting with others, our awareness centers directly and primarily on what we are doing, not on ourselves doing it. Though we are aware of ourselves in a general, unnamed sort of way, we are so wrapped up in what is happening that we do not sit back and self-consciously watch ourselves experience it. We are simply caught up in the flow of things. The same is true of good liturgy. When we gather together as God's people to listen to our God in faith and to take part in a covenanting action with God, our attention focuses directly on God's word and offer of covenant. There is a general awareness of ourselves, but we do not sit back and observe ourselves listening to the word or breaking the bread. In a real sense the experience is unobserved and inarticulate.

Attending to our liturgical experience requires, then, that we first have to recover it from its lived, unobserved state and relive it in some fashion. This can be readily done, it seems to me, in one of two ways. The experience can be recovered by some form of reminiscing. Powerful memories of meaningful liturgical actions are deeply embedded within us and surface easily. It only takes a relaxing, trusting setting and a lead question or two to revive the memories imprinted by the textures, colors, sounds, smells, and bodily movements and postures of the liturgy. This recovery can also be accomplished by isolating a particular gesture or symbolic action from its ritual setting and performing it together with care and attentiveness. Anointing the hands with fragrant oil, signing each other's foreheads with water, or setting the eucharistic table with care, each accompanied by a brief poetic reflection on the action or object, can readily evoke the liturgical experience in a reflective setting.

Describing the liturgical experience happens easily once that experience has been brought to the front of our consciousness in a reflective learning setting. In fact, the two often go hand in hand. One way of reminiscing, for example, is to describe what happened to us. By description I here mean a factual recounting of the physical, sensory experience, such as the darkness of the confessional box, the gentle and winsome quality of the songs and stories of Advent, the colors, textures and special practices of Lent, the physical discomfort of kneeling, or the foreign sound of Latin. This sort of description may at first seem unimportant, something to be passed over in favor of naming the inner, spiritual value of liturgical gestures and symbols. But it is precisely in and through their sensory, tactile dimensions that they tell us of the inner graces they convey to us. That is the way of sacraments. And so it is there that we must start.

We are not content with such bare description, however. We quickly feel a need to name the inner quality of our experience, the feelings and attitudes it evokes in us, the sense of ourselves and relationship to others and to the world around us subtly contained there. In naming the inner quality of the experience, we begin to uncover the fully human meaning which that experience bears for us. It is at this point that we are ready to move into the second step.

Reflecting. In this second step we now ask ourselves what the experience we have begun to name means. Again, as in the previous step, there are several interlocking things that happen.

As we relive our experience and try to name it for ourselves, we each begin to explore more fully what our experience can tell us about ourselves and our world. For example, what do the darkness and anonymity of the traditional confessional box tell us about God, about ourselves, about sin, about forgiveness? How do they suggest those things to us, and why? Or conversely, what does our experience of the new rite of reconciliation, where our self-disclosure is made face to face in the light, tell us about these same things? How? Why? Reflecting in this way we take the bits and pieces of our personal life experience and put them together into a larger, coherent whole. We have begun to decipher their meaning and fit them together as parts of our life story.

At this point it is important to hear one another's stories, to hear what the experience means for others. The mutual telling of our life stories is one of the most critical and effective ways of helping us understand both ourselves and others. Hearing another's story with understanding or entrusting our story to another enables us to see ourselves through that person's eyes. Such sharing, however, requires that we establish an atmosphere of mutual trust and respect, and it happens best in small groups. What we discover at this point is that our life stories have similar patterns and rhythms. A larger, common version begins to take shape around the common stuff of our lives.

For that larger story to be complete, we need to expand our exploration to include the story of those who have lived through these same experiences before us, whose ways and wisdom have shaped our world. Only in this way, when we set our experience alongside theirs, can we learn from them while yet respecting what our experience teaches us. For the christian community, which reaches back across the centuries to the Lord Jesus, it is finally only his story that can serve as the master story for us all, only his vision of the kingdom that can capture all we dare to envision.

For a fruitful dialogue with the wisdom and vision of the past to take place, it is important to have the help of a resource person who can tell us how that story has unfolded in the tradition of our people. Thus, to return to the example of reconciliation, we need to hear about Jesus' stories of forgiveness and his way of treating those broken by sin. We need to hear about how the early church gathered on Ash Wednesday to pray with penitents when they received ashes and entered on their once-in-a-lifetime lenten journey of penance; how they again gathered with the penitents on Holy Thursday to welcome them when they were absolved and re-admitted to the table. We need to hear about how the medieval Irish monks introduced a personal form of penance which could be celebrated repeatedly as a form of spiritual direction. Each of these are unique stories of how our people have found forgiveness and reconciliation. One who can tell us these stories helps us see our personal stories as part of something larger. And as we make that larger story our own, we are ready to move into the next step of the process.

Applying. In the final step we ask ourselves how what we have learned can shape the future, both for ourselves and for those who come after us. Without such follow-up, learning would remain nothing more than theory.

The obvious follow-up action is to take what we have learned and use it to shape our future celebration of the liturgy. For example, we might decide together that the confessionals need to be redone to encourage pastoral guidance, or that a lenten penitential process would bring a sense of solidarity and reconciliation to our community. Such follow-up actions can be done most effectively through a process of preparing and evaluating our celebrations in light of what we have learned. These two tasks will be the concern of the next chapter, so more need not be said about them here.

Overt action, however, is not the only way in which we apply our learning. This is particularly true in the case of liturgy. The first and perhaps most important benefit to be gained from our reflection on our experience of the liturgy is a heightened sensitivity to the way in which liturgy speaks to us. This cannot help but have an impact on our ability to participate in the liturgy. Thus, alert to the example of the Irish monks, we might find the inspiration to breathe new life into our own approach to the celebration of personal reconciliation, whether as penitent or minister. As we become more attentive to the symbolic ways of the liturgy, our capacity to speak its symbolic languages grows, and we become more susceptible to what the liturgy says to us.

Summary

1. Liturgical celebration has a formative influence of its own. Both the assembly and its ministers, however, have need of a more explicit liturgical catechesis to break open the liturgical gestures and symbols, so that they may understand and celebrate them more fully.

2. Liturgical catechesis should let its goals, learning styles, and content be shaped by the liturgy itself. Adult participation is the normative goal of liturgy; liturgical catechesis should aim toward the mature understanding required for such participation. Litur-

gy is the shared action of a community; liturgical instruction should provide a setting in which the community can reflect together on the meaning that action has for them. Through symbols that are rich in multiple meanings and oriented to building relationships, the liturgy expresses and enacts the meaning of our lives as God's people; liturgical catechesis should help us name and deepen our awareness and experience of being that holy people.

3. Relying on these principles and drawing on models of liturgical catechesis developed for the catechumenate in the ancient church and for adult religious education in today's church, we can sketch a method for liturgical catechesis. It is built on a three-step process of attending to what we actually experience at liturgy, reflecting on what our experience and that of the larger community means, and applying what we have learned to future celebration of the liturgy.

Notes

1. "With zeal and patience pastors must promote the liturgical instruction of the faithful and also their active participation in the liturgy both internally and externally, taking into account their age and condition, their way of life, and their stage of religious development."

2. For further reading, see: Robert L. Browning and Roy A. Reed, *The Sacraments in Religious Education and Liturgy: An Ecumenical Model* (Birmingham, AL: Religious Education Press, 1985); Thomas H. Groome, *Christian Religious Education. Sharing Our Story and Vision* (San Francisco: Harper & Row, 1980); Gwen Kennedy Neville and John H. Westerhoff III, *Learning Through Liturgy* (New York: Seabury Press, 1978); John H. Westerhoff III, *Will Our Children Have Faith?* (New York: Seabury Press, 1976).

3. For a thought-provoking look at the formative impact of liturgy see: Mark Searle, "The Pedagogical Function of the Liturgy," *Worship* 55 (1981) 332–359.

4. Groome's major work is *Christian Religious Education. Sharing Our Story and Vision* (San Francisco: Harper & Row, 1980). His thought is nicely summarized in an earlier article entitled "Christian Education: A Task of Present Dialectical Hermeneutics," *The Living Light* 14 (1977) 408–423.

5. An excellent example of how his method can be used in adult catechesis on the sacraments can be found in: Richard M. Gula, *To Walk Together Again. The Sacrament of Reconciliation* (New York: Paulist Press, 1984).

2

Preparing and Evaluating the Liturgy

SOONER OR LATER EVERY LITURGICAL CATECHIST EXPERIENCES the bitter disappointment of a liturgical celebration which does not deliver what the catechesis had promised. The lesson is hard, but clear. Catechesis for the liturgy is only the first phase in a cycle of pastoral care for God's people at prayer. That cycle must continue on into the preparation of the celebration and be completed by an evaluation of the celebration if the catechesis is to have any lasting effect.

But to take up the issues of planning and evaluating the liturgy is to enter poorly mapped or even uncharted territory. If we are to avoid getting lost in the myriad details and conflicting dos and don'ts we will be exploring, we need to keep our eyes fixed on the pastoral goal of planning and evaluating: serving God's people at prayer. Austin Fleming's bluntly worded advice, that we stop trying to *plan* the liturgy, as though we have to redesign it each time, and start *preparing* ourselves and the celebration instead,[1] can serve as our beacon. Preparing the liturgy is an art, a ministry. The same must be said for evaluating the celebration. These ministries, like any art, presume that we have acquired disciplined skills and move beyond them, using those skills to truly serve the people at prayer. As we try to explore and chart the issues at stake in preparing and evaluating liturgy, we need to continually look beyond the details and skills to God's people whose prayer they are meant to serve.

PREPARING THE LITURGY

Preparing the liturgy is still a very new experience for the contemporary church. Ways of going about it range all the way from leaving it to chance decisions made on the spot while the liturgy is in progress, to methodically following a set process of preparing and fully coordinating everything in advance in meticulous detail. The process usually falls somewhere in between these extremes, allowing individual liturgical ministers, such as the music director, to prepare their own area of responsibility with a certain minimum of communication and coordination. At times the preparation is marked by prayer and serious attention to both the special circumstances of the local congregation and the inherited shape and meaning of liturgical forms. At other times it is based on personal taste or whim.

Even if it were possible to reduce this welter of experience to one neat, universal system of preparing the liturgy, it would not be right to do so. The new liturgy requires preparation; it is not an optional frill. But in the end the concrete form the preparation takes must be specific to each community, its needs and resources, its liturgical style, and the leadership styles and liturgical expertise of its ministers and resource people. For that reason the observations offered here are only meant to be "generic," of use, it is hoped, for a variety of styles of going about it.[2] The observations are organized under a series of questions.

First, why must we prepare?

The need for preparation is rooted in the liturgical renewal set in motion by Vatican II. In keeping with its decision to restore active participation of the assembly, the Council called for a revision of the rites that would allow them to be adapted to peoples in their own cultures (CSL #38 [DOL #38]).[3]

The results of that revision are revealing. The new ritual books present us with an official, normative structure for each rite. Though complete, these official rites show significant flexibility. The rites typically offer a variety of alternate texts for prayers and readings; there are ritual options, and the new rubrics are often content to give no more than general descriptions of how a rite is to be done. The introduction to each rite normally calls attention to the need for pastoral adaptation of the rite to the circumstances and spiritual needs of the assembly and gives "guidelines" for "proper planning" of the celebration.[4] Rome itself provided us with an official adaptation of the eucharistic rite when it issued a directory for masses with children that outlines a broad range of adaptations that can be made when the assembly is composed entirely or significantly of children. Adapting the rites so that the assembly can participate actively and fully, in body and in spirit, clearly requires us to prepare the celebration (GIRM #3 [DOL #1393]; CSL #14 [DOL #14]).

And what is liturgical preparation?

Put simply, to prepare is to get ourselves and the rites ready for the celebration. Stated more elegantly, liturgical preparation is a regular process by which the standard forms and environment of a liturgical rite are fleshed out and adapted to the particular circumstances and spiritual needs of the assembly which gathers to celebrate it.

This idea of preparation flows from the comments made above about the normative, guideline character of the rites as scripted in the liturgical books. Preparation seeks to adapt the "standard model" of the liturgy to the assembly at hand, to adjust the liturgical symbols to the people to whom and for whom they are to speak. Such preparation has to follow a regular procedure to ensure fidelity to the normative liturgy and to the needs of the assembly, as well as continuity from celebration to celebration. The many ways in which the liturgy speaks to us, like a language, can not be learned from scratch each time; they thrive only when we are allowed to become fluent in them through repeated use. Constant experimenting or tinkering can easily lead a liturgy team to succumb to personal taste or whim and leave the assembly without any chance to make new ways of using the liturgical symbols its own. When all is said and done, our overriding pastoral responsibility is the spiritual needs and benefit of the assembly (GIRM #313 [DOL #1703]).

Who should do the preparing?

The recent documents on the liturgy are clear and consistent in naming those who should be involved (GIRM #313 [DOL #1703]; MCW #10, 12).

Involvement of the presider-homilist is a must. No other liturgical minister or member of the assembly is as critically important to the success of a celebration as the one whose role is to gather the assembly as one, break open the word for it, and lead its prayer. If our pastoral goal is to adapt the liturgy so that the people can hear God's word and pray in their real life situations, the presider-homilist must be there, to shape and be shaped by what is prepared. It is impossible to communicate in a few minutes what took an hour or more to germinate (MCW #12, 21).

But the presider is not the only one who must prepare. Responsibility also falls on "all who exercise major roles in the liturgy," write the U.S. bishops (MCW #10). Those who serve the assembly as its liturgical ministers cannot unite the assembly in prayer if they are not one in their understanding of the pastoral goals of a particular liturgical celebration and how it is to achieve those aims. Working together in preparing the liturgy is one of the best ways to forge liturgical ministers into a unified team. We have all witnessed the distracting and sometimes divisive effects of a disunified team of ministers. Caucuses called on the spot to instruct servers or to bring order into a chaotic situation may perhaps do no more than momentarily distract us from prayer. Open competition or reproach between ministers can totally destroy all prayer in the assembly. By contrast, if the ministers are openly of one mind and heart in serving the assembly and each other, their example calls the assembly to pray together in harmony.

Since it is the prayer and praise of the assembly that are to find voice in the liturgy, the assembly must also have a voice in preparing the celebration. There should be representatives of the assembly who are able to speak for the "diversity of ages, sexes, ethnic and cultural groups in the congregation" (EACW #30).

There is one final group whom we should enlist as resource persons in preparing the liturgy: men and women who are skilled in the arts and know what resources are available and who sense people's thirst to hear God's word and address God in prayer (MCW #12).

With the exception of the U.S. bishops' *Music in Catholic Worship*, these liturgical documents are less clear on how to coordinate the work and responsibilities of those who prepare the celebrations.

How is preparation to take place?

There are two questions here, one of structure, the other of procedures.

The structure we most commonly find in our parishes and communities is some form of liturgy committee or "planning" team. In their remarkable document on liturgical music the U.S. bishops call for just such a structure. After citing an official instruction which underlines the need for the cooperation of all concerned parties in making particular preparations for each liturgical celebration, the bishops go on to say: "In practice this ordinarily means an organized 'planning team' or committee which meets regularly to achieve creative and coordinated worship and a good use of the liturgical and musical options of a flexible liturgy" (MCW #10). They clearly envision something more than having individual ministers prepare in isolation.

Our experience of the past few years raises several questions and concerns regarding "planning" committees and their meeting patterns. The first, and perhaps most important, is Austin Fleming's question of perspective. We easily lose ourselves in the nuts and bolts of "planning" and begin to think of our task as one of designing the liturgy from scratch, rather than one of making ourselves, the rituals, the space, and the liturgical objects ready for the moment of public prayer.

Another critical item is that the committee structure needs to be tailored to each situation. Uncritically borrowing "the right way to do it" from another community can lead to much grief. So much of a committee's effectiveness depends on who the members are and how they work best together. Some committees thrive on consensus style. Others need someone who is clearly in charge, or a leader who will delegate responsibilities. Turnover in membership can easily skew a previously effective working style and necessitate restructuring. Such turnover, however, is something we should encourage, lest we overburden generous volunteers to the detriment of their home life or to the point of burnout.

The size of the committee is also a delicate issue. It is not always easy for a committee to find the balance between being unwieldy on the one hand and under-resourced on the other. Experience of unwieldy committees and overkill in preparation is leading some parishes to differentiate between the larger preparation required for an entire liturgical season, for example, and the more limited preparation needed for a particular celebration which will follow a familiar, established pattern. A larger committee is needed for the former; a small team may suffice for the latter.

Despite these concerns and caveats, however, the contribution of "planning" committees has been positive and essential to the renewal of the liturgy. At their best, such committees, because they draw a cross-section of the assembly into the process, more readily guarantee that the liturgy prepared for an assembly truly fits that assembly.

Procedures are a second part of the question of how to prepare liturgy.

The recommendation made above for structuring the group holds for its procedures as well. Each local committee would be well advised to covenant its own pastoral goals and procedures. Recent experience of liturgy committees alerts us to several distinctions and choices which each local group will have to make in their covenant.

It is important, first, to keep the distinction between planning and preparation in mind as the group defines its care and responsibilities for the community's public prayer.

It is also important for the committee to distinguish between the actual work of preparing specific celebrations and the larger tasks of setting pastoral goals for the liturgical life of the community, determining overall policies for the liturgy, and laying out regular procedures for liturgy preparation. A committee's work can become helplessly bogged down if these two levels of responsibility are not kept distinct. For example, having to decide each week who can be asked to read the scriptures, who appoints the servers, or whether the pastor will allow physical re-arrangement of furnishings to create special environments, can push a volunteer committee's patience and good will to the limit. The committee might decide to handle both areas, but keep them separate on the agenda. Or it might choose to keep only the larger tasks for itself and hand the work of actually preparing liturgies over to one or more working teams responsible to the committee.

Similarly, many committees are finding it helpful to distinguish between preparing the celebrations for a particular Sunday and preparing entire seasons or larger segments of the church year. After the Council we began with the short-term approach, "planning" Sunday by Sunday. Preparing a series of celebrations at the same time is now coming into its own. This allows us to take more account of spirit and motifs that mark a season, for example, or of the unique perspectives and concerns woven through a particular book of the scriptures which is read over a series of Sundays. The local committee may choose, as some do, to assign this larger kind of preparation to itself. Smaller working teams can then be delegated to apply this larger vision to the particular celebrations of a given Sunday.

Each committee or team will also have to find the way of conducting preparation meetings that suits it best. Experience suggests several important components: 1) sharing a moment of prayer, 2) listening to the scripture readings together to lift out graphic images or phrases that resonate with what people are experiencing, 3) attending with the homilist to how the readings might be broken open, and with musicians, ritual performers, and environmental artists to how the liturgy's meaning for that day can be harmoniously embodied for those who will assemble, and 4) making sure that follow-up responsibilities are clearly delegated.

There are numerous pastoral aids available to help a liturgy committee structure itself and organize its work.[5]

Once the basic preparation is in place, the committee's task of getting a celebration ready concludes with monitoring the preparation of individual ministers and arranging for practice sessions and rehearsals as needed, to ensure proper coordination and to make any needed revisions. The committee's work resumes after the celebration with its task of evaluating the results.

EVALUATING THE LITURGY

The task of evaluating the celebrations we have prepared receives no attention in liturgical documents, apart from a passing mention in the U.S. bishops' statement on liturgical music (MCW #12). Perhaps that lack of an official church call explains why the practice of evaluating our liturgies seems so sporadic and casual compared to time we spend preparing them. But evaluation provides the critical finishing touch to the whole preparation process and deserves to be taken far more seriously. The following brief remarks about evaluation are offered as starters for your consideration. They are framed by the same questions used for preparation.

First, why should we evaluate the liturgy?

Two reasons can be cited. Vatican II stressed that it is the duty of those who have responsibility for the liturgy "to ensure that the faithful take part fully aware of what they are doing, actively engaged in the rite, and enriched by its effects" (CSL #11 [DOL #11]). This surely implies some sort of follow-up assessment.

Furthermore, the very reason for preparing celebrations is to help a local assembly gradually develop a liturgical style adapted to its circumstances and spiritual needs. If the fruits of successful preparation are to be carried over from one celebration to the next, evaluation provides the natural bridge. It completes the cycle by sorting out what was effective or ineffective in what we did and enables us to enter the next cycle of catechesis/preparation with that self-critical knowledge at our disposal.

What, then, is evaluation of the liturgy like?

Evaluation is not just relying on the chance reports or first impressions we pick up afterwards from members of the assembly or from the liturgy committee. These are important, but they may be too piecemeal or may too easily reflect vested interests to give us a balanced view. Rather, evaluation that is worthy of the name must be a regular process of serious reflection on the pastoral choices and adaptations we have made, in order to assess both their effectiveness in adjusting the liturgy to the needs of the assembly and their usefulness for future celebrations.

Who should do the evaluating?

It is right that those who were involved in preparing the celebration should also evaluate it. While others may have noted the choices and adaptations made in preparing the liturgy, only those who did the preparing are fully aware of all the pastoral considerations and goals that lay behind those choices and adaptations. Asking them to do a serious evaluation of their work puts the final touch on their responsibility.

Those who exercised major ministerial roles in the celebration serve an equally important role in the evaluation process, especially if they were not on the preparation team. Like performers in a play, they have a unique perspective on the liturgical experience that its designers may not have.

It is possible, however, for both committee and principal performers to mistake their intent for the actual accomplishment. For that reason, as the bishops point out when they talk about the composition of "planning committees" in their document on music in worship, "It is always good to include some members of the congregation who have not taken special roles in the celebrations so that honest evaluations can be made" (MCW #12). This is, finally, the acid test of the success of a celebration. Did it enable the assembly to hear God's word, to praise, to pray? Only members of the assembly can tell us that.

How should we go about evaluating the liturgy?

First, make it a practice to begin each meeting of the liturgy committee or team with an evaluation of the last celebration they prepared. If a long time intervenes, members might be encouraged to record their impressions, assessment, and follow-up questions as soon as possible after the celebration. A form can be developed to facilitate this. Their own familiarity with the preparations gives them a unique perspective from which to do the evaluation.

Second, collect assessments from liturgical ministers with major roles and from some members of the congregation. Though this can be done orally, it is better to do it in writing. A form, one page at most, that is inviting and easy to fill out is an ideal way. An effectively constructed form might include two kinds of categories, one asking people to rate each of a list of qualities the committee sought in preparing the liturgy, the other inviting them to write down what helped or hindered their prayer, or what they commend (positive) or recommend (negative, to be revised). Members of the assembly could be asked to serve as the liturgy "Nielsen rating sample" on a regular basis. The entire congregation might occasionally be invited to fill out the form. Periodic open forum meetings with the liturgy committee and pastoral staff offer another means.

These procedures may sound forbidding if we have not done evaluations until now. In that case it might be wise to ease our way into it gradually, as we'll suggest in a moment. The important point is that the liturgy committees find a reliable way to hear honest feedback from the assembly and that the committee give these reports serious consideration.

KEEPING OUR BEARINGS

Lest we lose our bearings amidst the welter of details and ideas we have been exploring for preparing and evaluating liturgy, we need to return to our opening word of caution about keeping a proper perspective. Preparing and evaluating liturgy are moments of caring for God's people at prayer. Keeping the people's spiritual needs and their participation as our foremost pastoral concerns is our surest defense against letting these moments of ministry wander off into excessive concern for externals and mechanics. This is the first and most important bit of advice we need to take to heart.

Second, we need to keep preparation and evaluation of our celebrations inseparably linked together. Preparation that is not critiqued leaves us unsure of both our successes and our failures in caring for the people's prayer; critique that has no constructive outlet back into the preparation process leaves us frustrated and powerless to either correct failures or build on the successes.

Third, preparation has had a head start and needs to wait for evaluation to catch up. To the extent that we find ourselves trapped in the kind of frenetic planning Austin Fleming warns us about, this may be a welcome moment of grace. While we go about learning the art of evaluating liturgical celebrations, we can do two things to both simplify and improve our preparation of the people's prayer: we can concentrate on the primary ritual actions, words, and objects, rather than lavish indiscriminate attention on every least detail; and we can refocus from mechanics and details onto the basic spirit and motifs of seasons or larger segments of the church year.

Fourth, we need to develop effective ways of evaluating our celebrations, even if it means starting from scratch. Our experience with the earlier style of "planning" liturgy has a valuable lesson to teach us. Would it not be wisest to start simply and build up gradually, using the focal points we stressed in preparing the liturgy? Major feasts and seasons offer us ideal times to start, given the importance we attach to preparing and celebrating them. In the beginning it would also help to concentrate on what is more central and important in our prayer, ritual action and objects, and environment.

One further element has to be added to each of these last two points, but that will be the task of the next chapter.

Summary

1. Preparation is needed to adapt the "standard" liturgical rites to the circumstances and spiritual needs of each assembly. There should be a regular preparation process involving the presider, the major liturgical ministers and musicians, artists, and representatives of the assembly. They normally work together in liturgy committees or teams, each covenanting their pastoral goals, structures, and procedures.

2. Evaluating the liturgy is the necessary complement to responsible preparation, a final step in the process. Evaluation

assesses whether the pastoral adaptations made in preparing the celebration were effective and of continuing benefit for the assembly. Both the liturgy committee and members of the assembly should do the evaluating.

3. A unified pastoral program of preparing and evaluating our celebrations will focus on the primary seasons and elements of celebration. It will start simply and grow in response to its pastoral effectiveness and usefulness. The participation of the people and their spiritual good will be its ultimate norm and goal.

Notes

1. Austin Fleming, *Preparing for Liturgy. A Theology and Spirituality* (Washington, D.C.: The Pastoral Press, 1985), 31–41. This book is must reading for everyone who prepares liturgy or serves on a liturgy committee. In keeping with his stress that our ways of naming things influence how we think of them, I have tried to use language of "preparing" in place of the more familiar "planning" throughout this book.

2. Among the many fine resources available for further reading on "planning" structures and procedures, see: Thomas Baker and Frank Ferrone, *Liturgy Committee Basics. A No-Nonsense Guide* (Washington, D.C.: The Pastoral Press, 1985); Fred Krause, *Liturgy in Parish Life. A Study of Worship and the Celebrating Community* (New York: Alba House, 1979), 161–179; Marty Meyer, *Goal Setting for Liturgy Teams* (Chicago: Liturgy Training Publications, 1981); Mark Searle, *Liturgy Made Simple* (Collegeville: Liturgical Press, 1981), 75–95.

3. For further reading on liturgical adaptation, see: Anscar Chupungco, *Cultural Adaptation of the Liturgy* (New York: Paulist Press, 1982).

4. Thus GIRM #6 (DOL #1396): "The purpose of this Instruction is to give the general guidelines for planning the eucharistic celebration properly..."

5. Among the more reflective and "wholistic" resources I might cite: Yvonne Cassa and Joanne Sanders, *Groundwork: Planning Liturgical Seasons* (Chicago: Liturgy Training Publications, 1982); Dennis J. Geaney and Dolly Sokol, *Parish Celebrations. A Reflective Guide for Liturgy Planning* (Mystic, CT: Twenty-Third Publications, 1983); Gabe Huck, *Liturgy with Style and Grace* (Chicago: Liturgy Training Publications, 1984).

3

Establishing Qualities and Criteria

THE LAST CHAPTER LEFT UNTOUCHED WHAT ARE PERHAPS THE knottiest questions facing those who prepare and evaluate liturgy. What makes a liturgy a good liturgy? What qualities should we work for in our liturgy? By what criteria are we to judge whether or not a liturgy was pastorally successful? How does one go about establishing these qualities and criteria?

It comes as no surprise that liturgists and liturgy committees wrestling with these questions have come up with a variety of answers.[1] And perhaps that is as it should be, given what we have been saying here about the uniqueness of each pastoral situation in which the liturgy is celebrated. Selecting and prioritizing the qualities and criteria for liturgies that are appropriate to the community it serves is something each liturgy committee has to do for itself. The time and energy spent in establishing and implementing a working set of qualities and criteria might end up being one of the single most important things a liturgy committee can do. It forces us to go beyond a superficial, technician's approach to the liturgy and to address the deeper issue of what our pastoral goals are in preparing and evaluating liturgical celebrations.

My intent in this chapter is to provide working materials for that task rather than a ready-made formula. The materials will be of a general kind, with more particular suggestions to follow in part two, and will be summarized first from the liturgical documents and then from my own point of view. The materials will also seem massive. They are presented only as idea-starters. A committee will have to select a few as its priorities, perhaps starting with one or two at a time.

MINING THE OFFICIAL DOCUMENTS

There are three documents to which we can turn for help in our efforts to establish the qualities and criteria for a good liturgy. The first of these is Vatican II's *Constitution on the Sacred Liturgy*. Chapter one of the Constitution concludes with several sets of norms to be implemented in the liturgical revisions. These norms offer some helpful guidelines for our questions.

One such set of norms (CSL #26-32 [DOL #26-32]) identifies several qualities which are to characterize the new liturgy. The liturgy should be celebrated communally by an assembly, rather than in private. The assembly should be fully, consciously, and actively engaged in the celebration. The various liturgical roles should be distributed within the assembly and all members of the assembly should be allowed to exercise their proper roles without infringement.

Another group of norms (CSL #33-36 [DOL #33-36]) reaffirms a historic set of qualities that have been part of the genius of the roman rite since ancient times. In a passage often quoted in answer to the question of what qualities to look for in a liturgy, the constitution says: "The rites should be marked by a noble simplicity; they should be short, clear, and unencumbered by useless repetitions; they should be within the people's powers of comprehension and as a rule not require much explanation" (CSL #34 [DOL 34]).

A final set of norms (CSL #37-40 [DOL #37-40]) calls the church to both preserve the substantial unity of the roman rite and adapt it to the local cultures of peoples.

The second document which furnishes us with useful material is the U.S. bishops' *Music in Catholic Worship*, cited earlier. The third section of that document (MCW #23-41) outlines three judgments which are to guide planners in selecting music for a celebration. The *musical judgment* asks whether the piece is good musical art. The *liturgical judgment* asks whether that piece can also serve the liturgy, since good art does not automatically make good liturgical art. The *pastoral judgment* asks whether that which is good liturgical music in itself suits the particular assembly and occasion for which it will be used. The committee must be able to answer all three questions in the affirmative. These three judgments could easily be made to serve as criteria for every symbolic form used in the liturgy.

The final document which has much to offer toward our discussion is another one issued by the U.S. bishops, *Environment and Art in Catholic Worship*. Its first section on the requirements of worship (EACW #9–26) is particularly helpful. The bishops write that the liturgy should be traditional, yet contemporary; it should express both human hospitality and the mystery of God; it should be a personal-communal experience. They call for a manner of celebrating which opens up our symbols. Art forms, they say, are to serve the liturgy and should be marked by quality and appropriateness.

Together these documents offer a wealth of ideas from which we can draw in setting down our lists of qualities and criteria. They deserve our careful and thoughtful reading.

MAPPING THE QUALITIES AND CRITERIA

How can we pull together in managable form what these and similar documents, as well as our growing experience, teach us about what to look for as we prepare and evaluate liturgy? It may be of help to organize them using a three-fold schema employed by anthropologists in studying rituals: the performers of the ritual, the structure of the ritual, and the ritual symbols and actions. I offer this schematization as a second set of working materials to help sort through the question of qualities and criteria. The materials are purposely very detailed in order to stir ideas; an actual working list would contain no more than a few qualities and criteria, chosen as priorities because of their particular importance for our assemblies.

A word about the layout. Each section of the schema begins with a basic norm. The qualities to prepare for and evaluate in a good liturgy are then given in italics with a brief explanation. Finally, evaluation questions are interspersed for each quality, and summary questions attempt to focus larger areas of concern. These questions could be easily recast for use in preparing as well. References to documents are included for those who wish to study the sources further.

PERFORMERS OF THE LITURGY

The assembly

Norm: Communal celebration of the liturgy is the norm. The primary criterion of good liturgy is the full, active, conscious participation of the assembly (CSL #14 [DOL #14]).[2]

Prepare and evaluate:

1. *Full participation.* Ministers who see the liturgy as their personal action and, however graciously or grudgingly, allow the assembly to assist do not observe this norm. Full participation means that the assembly not only takes an active part, but that the liturgy is truly theirs. It also means that those who prepare the liturgy are to consult the assembly and adapt the celebration to their culture, circumstances, and spiritual needs. Evaluation question: Was the liturgy truly the assembly's action?

2. *Active participation.* The active participation called for by Vatican II is not merely external activity, but a participation that engages the mind and spirit by engaging the body and its senses. Were members of the assembly fully and actively engaged in body and spirit?

3. *Conscious participation.* To use an alternate phrasing of Vatican II, this means that the assembled people are to take part in the liturgy "fully aware of what they are doing." There are two levels to this awareness. First, people are to be fully aware of doing the liturgy. They are entitled to adequate instruction and preparation beforehand and to restrained, unobtrusive explanations and participation aids during the liturgy so that they can understand and follow the rites. Second, and more importantly, they are to be fully aware of doing the liturgy as God's people. The celebration should enable the people, gathered to hear God's word and to renew covenant, to sense God's presence and workings in their lives, to know themselves as God's people and followers of Jesus Christ, called to witness and spread the kingdom through their lives. Did the assembly take part fully aware of what they were doing?

Summary question: Did the assembly hear the word of God, pray, and offer praise?

The ministers

Norm: "In liturgical celebrations each one, minister or layperson, who has an office to perform, should do all of, but only, those parts which pertain to that office by the nature of the rite and the principles of liturgy" (CSL #28 [DOL #28]).[3]

Prepare and evaluate:

4. *Variety of roles.* Well ordered liturgy requires that various roles be filled by ordained ministers, special ministers, and members of the assembly. Were the various liturgical roles distributed and respected?

5. *Adequate preparation.* Those who exercise liturgical ministries are to be "trained to perform their functions in a correct and orderly manner" (CSL #29 [DOL #29]) and informed of their responsibilities beforehand "so that nothing is improvised" (GIRM #313 [DOL #1703]). Were the ministers prepared?

6. *Effective performance.* Effective liturgy depends on the human naturalness, the respectful care, and the prayerfulness of those who minister. Did the ministers perform their roles effectively?

Summary question: Did the ministers serve the assembly?

STRUCTURE OF THE LITURGY

The overall pattern

Norm: The integrity of a liturgical celebration requires that it preserve the substantial unity of the roman rite while allowing for legitimate variations and adaptations to different groups, regions, and peoples, and that the harmonious interconnections of its parts be maintained (CSL #37–38, 50, [DOL #37–38, 50]; GIRM #8 [DOL #1398]).

Prepare and evaluate:

7. *Integrity of structure.* Was the liturgy celebrated with fidelity to the structure of the roman rite and to the culture and spiritual needs of the assembly?

8. *Proper value given each part.* Not all parts of a liturgy are of equal importance. For example, in the mass the introductory and concluding rites are of secondary importance compared to the liturgy of the word and the liturgy of the eucharist (MCW #43). Was the relative importance of each part respected?

9. *Rhythm and balance.* Effective liturgy is marked by rhythm, balance, and movement between the parts, so that the assembly experiences moments of intensity and relaxation and a buildup to properly chosen peaks, such as the Gospel, great amen, and communion, as it moves through the rite. Was there proper rhythm, balance, and movement between the various parts?

Summary question: Did the liturgy catch the people up in its flow - gathering them, feeding them on God's word, uncovering the experience of dying and rising with Christ at the core of their daily lives, and sending them forth renewed?

The component parts

Norm: The integrity of a liturgical celebration requires that it respect the intrinsic nature and pastoral purpose of each part (CSL #50 [DOL #50]; GIRM #24-57 (DOL #1414-1447); MCW #42-49)[4] while making judicious use of the variations and alternatives provided in the rite for the spiritual good of the assembly.

Prepare and evaluate:

10. *Integrity of each part.* Integrity is less a matter of doing a literal rendition of rubric and text than it is of fulfilling the intrinsic nature and pastoral purpose of each part. For example, the *Directory for Masses with Children* (#24 [DOL

#2157]) provides that another adult may be allowed to give the homily if the presider finds it difficult to adapt himself to the mentality of the children, on the principle that it is of greater pastoral importance that the word be preached effectively to the children than that the normal regulations regarding homilists be observed. That directory contains many similar examples. Were each of the component parts (gathering, word, sacrament, sending) celebrated with fidelity to the roman rite and to the culture and the spiritual needs of the assembly?

11. *Proper value of each element.* Not every element within a given part of the liturgy is of equal importance. For example, the primary elements of the preparation rite are the bringing of the gifts, the placing of them on the altar, and the prayer over the gifts. All other elements are secondary (MCW #46). Clearly the primary elements are the ones we should plan to enhance with song and special ritual care. Was the relative importance of each element respected?

12. *Pastoral adaptations and variations.* Variations and alternate ways of doing the rite (e.g. the alternate readings, prayers, and presidential introductions provided in the various parts of the rite) are there to be *used*. Was there responsible and effective pastoral use of the variety of options?

Summary question: Did each part of the liturgy serve its pastoral purpose?

SYMBOLIC LANGUAGES AND SYMBOLS OF THE LITURGY

The many symbolic languages and symbols

Norm: Just as the human reality of Jesus mediates God's presence to us, so too our bodily actions and use of human objects in the liturgy tangibly express and bring about God's sanctifying presence to us and our worship of God in spirit and truth. Liturgical celebration depends radically on the honest use of the full range of symbolic languages and liturgical symbols. These "signs perceptible to the human senses" either nourish or destroy faith by the way in which they are performed. Full participation thus involves both the spirit and the body in all its senses (CSL #7 [DOL #7]; GIRM #5 [DOL #1395]; MCW #1-9; EACW #13).

Prepare and evaluate:

13. *Variety of symbols, symbolic languages.* Each liturgical language or symbol, such as silence, posture, ritual gesture, song, and season, communicates the mystery of God's presence in its own unique way. No one of them should be reduced to being a mere illustration for another of the languages, such as the spoken word; each should be allowed to speak in its own way. Were the various liturgical symbols and symbolic languages used fully, with respect for their uniqueness?

14. *Balance and harmony.* Ritual communication in liturgy, as in all cases of human interaction, shows an interplay and redundancy between the various languages being used. Were the liturgical symbols and languages balanced and in harmony in what they said to the assembly?

15. *Full embodiment.* Ritual communication in liturgy, like all human ritual communication, is based on bodily interaction and makes use of all the senses, especially touch, sight, and hearing. A liturgy which treats us as disembodied spirits denies our wholeness. Was the liturgy fully embodied, especially by the liturgical ministers?

Summary question: Did the liturgical symbols and languages together speak to and for the assembly, nourishing their faith and lives?

The artistic quality

Norm: Every liturgical symbol or ritual action must have an artistic quality. Liturgy takes its inspiration for symbol and ritual action from the fine arts, both visual arts and performing arts, and welcomes the artistic expressions, both folk and classic, of past ages and of contemporary peoples, when they are able to serve the liturgy beautifully and worthily (CSL #122-124 [DOL #122-124]; GIRM #253-254 [DOL #1643-1644]; EACW #18).

Prepare and evaluate:

16. *Simple and attractive beauty of objects.* Liturgical objects are to possess a quality that bespeaks both an honesty and genuineness of materials and the artist's care and gift in crafting them with a special touch (EACW #12, 20). Did the liturgical symbols possess a simple and attractive beauty and show the artist's hand?

17. *Noble simplicity of rites.* In design, "the rites should be marked by a noble simplicity; they should be short, clear, and unencumbered by useless repetitions; they should be within the people's powers of comprehension and as a rule not require much explanation" (CSL #34 [DOL #34]; EACW #17). Did the celebration possess a noble simplicity?

18. *Effective performance/use.* In the liturgy ritual actions should be performed and liturgical objects used in a way that is humanly attractive, natural, and invitational, and with a care and attentiveness that makes the ritual moment special (MCW #7, 9, 21; EACW #11-12). Were ritual actions performed and liturgical objects used effectively?

Summary question: Did the liturgy appeal to the senses?

The liturgical quality

Norm: Every ritual action or symbolic object used in the liturgy must be appropriate to the liturgy, possessing a transparency that invites the assembly to experience its God and itself as God's people (EACW #21-22, 12).

Prepare and evaluate:

19. *Liturgical appropriateness.* "The work of art must be appropriate in two ways: 1) it must be capable of bearing the weight of mystery, awe, reverence, and wonder

which the liturgical action expresses; 2) it must clearly *serve* (and not interrupt) ritual action which has its own structure, rhythm and movement" (EACW #21; also #22, 25). Were the symbolic objects and ritual actions appropriate to the liturgy?

20. *Multivocal symbols and ritual expressions.* Symbols and symbolic actions are by nature capable of bearing many meanings. Liturgical symbols should not be excessively restricted, especially by explanatory words, in what they can mean for the assembly. Were the multiple meanings of the symbols and symbolic actions respected?

21. *Fidelity to tradition and contemporary culture.* Liturgical symbols and symbolic actions are to speak in a tongue ever ancient and ever new. Were they faithful to tradition and to contemporary cultural expressions of the assembly?

Summary question: Did the liturgical symbols and actions serve the people and invite them to experience the unspeakable mystery of God?

The pastoral quality

Norm: The spiritual good of the assembled people is the final pastoral criterion for all effective planning and celebration of the liturgy (GIRM #313 [DOL #1703]).

Prepare and evaluate:

22. *Effective vehicles of communication.* Since liturgical symbols and ritual languages are all "vehicles of communication" (MCW #7), it is impossible for them not to convey something to the assembly. "Good celebrations foster and nourish faith. Poor celebrations may weaken and destroy it" (MCW #6). What did the celebration communicate to the assembled people?

23. *Opening up of symbols.* The renewed liturgy "requires the opening up of our symbols, especially the fundamental ones of bread and wine, water, oil, the laying on of hands, until we can experience all of them as

authentic and appreciate their symbolic value" (EACW #15). Were the liturgical actions and symbols opened up to the assembly?

24. *Fidelity to the assembly.* The pastoral effectiveness of a liturgy depends on the degree to which the liturgy is adapted to the culture, way of life, circumstances, and religious development of the people actually assembled to celebrate it. Was the celebration faithful to their spiritual needs?

Summary question: "People in love make signs of love" (MCW #4); did the celebration enable those present to express their love for God and each other?

SELECTING QUALITIES AND CRITERIA

A wide, detailed array of qualities and criteria have been purposely presented in the above outline to serve as idea starters for us. It is obvious we cannot work on all these qualities and criteria at the same time in preparing and evaluating liturgy. A selection has to be made for our individual pastoral situations. The few remarks which follow are offered as a help to guide us in that selection.

First, as the summary evaluation questions have tried to insist, our primary pastoral concern must always be to care for God's people at prayer. Their full and active participation must be the primary norm we follow in preparing and evaluating the celebration, their spiritual good must be the final goal of all our caring for their prayer.

Second, we need to develop a set of priorities which enfleshes that orientation to the assembly. We might, for example, make our own the three factors, listed earlier, which seem critical in enabling the assembly to feel at home in the celebration and to worship and pray. One is a fidelity to the assembly, both its liturgical tradition and the spiritual needs and life-situation of its members, a fidelity which tells us that the celebration is truly "ours." Another is the reverent care with which the central liturgical actions and symbols are prepared and performed/used, a care which tells us that what we do is a holy sacrament. A third is the obvious, contagious prayerfulness of those assembled, especially the ministers.

Third, we need to start small, selecting a few qualities and criteria to guide our preparation and evaluation in manageable ways. Thus, we might focus, one by one, on central ministerial actions which call for a congregational response, such as the reading of scriptures, the musical exchanges within the assembly, or the breaking and distribution of the eucharistic bread. Or again, we might take major feasts and seasons as an opportunity to attend to how we are using music and environment to heighten the assembly's sense of festivity. We might follow the example of one parish which has taken the qualities of hospitality and prayerfulness as the criteria on which celebrations are evaluated.

A final, sobering reminder is called for, lest we harbor impossible expectations about what we are to accomplish in caring for the people at prayer. In the end, all we can do is provide an atmosphere and an invitation to prayer and praise. The results depend on God's grace and each one's response. We cannot produce the inner prayer and praise on command.

Summary

1. Both preparing and evaluating celebrations depend on an awareness of what makes a liturgy pastorally effective for the assembly. A working set of qualities and criteria can be gleaned from the church's documents on liturgy which have shaped our experience of the renewed liturgy.

2. A detailed study outline of those qualities and criteria from the perspective of the performers, structures, and ritual symbols of the liturgy can stir our own ideas and help us reflect more carefully on the qualities we seek in a liturgy that is pastorally effective for our people.

3. In selecting the qualities and criteria we wish to stress, we should start small, set our priorities, and keep the full, active, and conscious participation of each particular assembly as our primary norm and their spiritual good as our ultimate pastoral goal.

Notes

1. The few resources available on evaluation are relatively brief. See, for example: Leonel L. Mitchell, *Liturgical Change. How Much Do We Need?* (New York: Seabury Press, 1975), 16–21.

2. See also: CSL #11, 19, 26–27, 30 (DOL #11, 19, 26–27, 30); GIRM #1–6 (DOL #1391–1396); MCW #15–18; EACW #27–38.

3. See also: CSL #29, 58 (DOL #29, 58); GIRM #59–61, 65–73 (DOL #1449–1451, 1455–1463); MCW #10–14, 21–22, 33–38; EACW #37.

4. See also: Sacred Congregation of Rites, *Musicam Sacram* #11 (DOL #4132).

4

Caring for God's People at Prayer

IN THE PRECEDING CHAPTERS WE HAVE REFLECTED AT LENGTH on liturgical catechesis, preparation, and evaluation. It is now time to gather up some of the central themes of those reflections, situate them in a vision of the liturgy and liturgical ministry, and weave them into a proposal for a pastoral program of caring for God's people at prayer. The vision we seek is not something we have to create; we have already discovered its most important features in our experience of the new liturgy and need only name them.

THE PEOPLE AT PRAYER

"We feel that the liturgy is ours now." That is a sentiment we hear voiced more and more as the new liturgy takes root.[1] And what an apt assessment it is! This new awareness that the liturgy is our action is one of the most important things we have discovered in the liturgical renewal. It stems from two Vatican II directives - that an assembly is to be present for the celebration of the liturgy whenever possible (CSL #27 [DOL #27]),[2] and that a full, conscious, and active participation of the gathered people is their baptismal right and duty (CSL #14 [DOL #14]).[3]

Our experience also tells us that the simple, unvarying components of every sacramental liturgy - gathering, word, action, sending - are dialogic or interactive. Each assumes a relationship between members of the assembly, and demands mutuality of the partners in that relationship.

Thus, gathering implies invitation and response, one who summons and those who are summoned. Sending happens only if someone sends and others are sent, giving and accepting a commission. Word breaks the silence that distances people and serves to link speaker and listener in sharing ideas, memories, and feelings as they constantly exchange roles while conversing. Actions invite reaction, which in turn triggers reaction of its own, and thus an episode unfolds as the interaction mounts and grows, actor and reactor locked together in a cycle of ever-reversing roles.

This rhythmic exchange is the basis on which our liturgy is built, and it cannot happen unless we each play our distinct roles in the assembly. Listening and speaking, giving and receiving, for example, take place only when dialogue partners each play their unique roles. We are learning to distribute and respect these roles as the Council mandated (CSL #28 [DOL #28]).[4] Liturgy, then, is something to be done together by an assembly of people in a dialogue of mutual service. This is another important discovery we have made, thanks to the liturgical reform.

That dialogue is not something we carry on between ourselves alone; God has become a partner in all we say and do in the assembly. There occurs in the liturgy what the doctors of the ancient church loved to call a "marvelous, holy exchange." Both sides of this exchange are voiced and embodied in the words and gestures we use in the liturgy. Human words and deeds become the symbols which mutually express God's self-disclosure and self-giving and our faith-hearing and giving over of ourselves to be filled and transformed by God. In the liturgy God and we keep covenant.

When we gather for liturgy, we find no better way to keep covenant than to tell and enact the story of Jesus, whose dying and rising sealed the covenant anew, once and for all. His dying and rising were at one and the same time God's offer of forgiveness and friendship to us and our acceptance of that offer. Completely one with God and with us, Jesus was the perfect go-between for us in our estrangement. In his paschal mystery Jesus revealed the human face of God and the transformed face of humanity. Jesus has pioneered our reunion with God and brought it to completion.

Jesus in his paschal mystery stands at the center of our celebration. The people he has made his own by the outpouring of the Spirit now join him in that pioneer journey of dying and rising, gradually making the paschal mystery more and more our own. When the people gather together to celebrate that paschal event in a moment of liturgy, Jesus is in our midst as our pioneer and liturgist, as he is named in Hebrews 12:2 and 8:2, enabling us to make that event our own. We remember his dying and rising, enter into it, and anticipate the time when it will be completed in us as it has been in Jesus.

As we experience more and more fully that Christ is presiding in all we do in our liturgical assembly, we are beginning to understand the meaning of a statement which the Council borrowed from Pius XII: "...in the liturgy the whole public worship is performed by the Mystical Body of Jesus Christ, that is by the Head and his members" (CSL #7 [DOL #7]). Our experience finds an even more graphic expression in 2 Corinthians 1:18-22. There Paul uses the image of a "yes" to make his point. Jesus is a single, two-way "yes" - God's "yes" to us and our human family's "yes" to God. Jesus continues to voice and embody that "yes" in the words and deeds of our liturgical celebrations. Liturgy is the action of the assembly, an action which bears within it the saving event of Christ.

What we have discovered in our experience of the renewed liturgy can be named thus: we have come to know the liturgy as our action which unfolds in the form of a many-layered dialogue and embodies within it the saving word and deed of God in Jesus Christ. These are the key features of a shining new vision of the liturgy. But we also experience a dark shadow in that vision. If we are honest, must we not also admit that our celebrations sometimes fall short of that vision?

The vision which our experience reveals challenges us in a number of ways. It establishes the pastoral goal and norm for all that we do in liturgical ministry. "This full and active participation by all the people," according to Vatican II, "is the aim to be considered before all else" (CSL #14 [DOL #14]). It also demands that we care for the people at prayer by providing the catechesis, spiritual preparation, and cared-for celebration they need and deserve.

CARING FOR THE PEOPLE AT PRAYER

A vision of what it means to be a liturgical minister also begins to emerge from our experience of the past two decades. Since the Vatican Council we have come to take a variety of liturgical ministers for granted, both those who serve us during the celebration and those who care for our prayer in other ways - liturgy committees and planning teams, directors of liturgy, conductors of adult and continuing education in liturgy, environmental artists, and diocesan consultants for liturgical space design.[5]

Many features of that experience are obvious and need only be named: the servant quality of liturgical ministry; the oneness of ministers with the assembly from which they come forth to minister and to which they return; the importance of their role in making us feel that the liturgy is ours. What is less noticed, however, is the subtle shift of focus that has taken place as these ministries have developed.

First, the inner meaning of the ministerial function and the spiritual preparation of the person of the minister have replaced the mechanics of catechesis, planning, and ritual performance as the focus of our concern.

Think, for instance, of how programs for lectors have evolved. We began with "training" programs which included segments on theology, but the key sessions were those on what to do and how to do it. Slowly our programs began to look beyond the techniques of the role to a deeper appreciation of its meaning. We felt a hunger for "something more" to sustain us. Theology workshops, prayer days and retreats, support groups, and various ways to build and sustain a ministerial spirituality appeared for lectors and, indeed, for all liturgical ministers.

Second, a change has occurred in how we recruit ministers. Embodying the meaning of the ministry is becoming more important than performing the externals. At first we enlisted whomever we could to fill out the ranks of ministers - the old reliables, the pillars of the parish; now we have begun to ask new questions.

Should not ministers of hospitality be welcoming persons who mirror the inclusiveness of the God who gathers us? Should not readers be listening people who hear and wrestle with the word in their own lives, so that we can overhear their faith in the reading? Should not communion ministers who offer us the One who is bread for the life of the world be in the process of becoming such bread themselves? And should not those who lead us in prayer and sacramental gesture be people who, like us, come with a painful awareness of their own neediness and with open arms, so that we can resonate with what they say and do? Should not a catechist be one who is wise in the community's ways of praying, rather than one who knows many things *about* liturgy? What we seek in a liturgical minister is not so much a functionary as one who has the gift of being a caring, ministering person in the service he or she performs.

The pattern in these developments may be faint, but it is discernible. From mechanics, to inner meaning and spiritual preparation, to awareness that a liturgical minister is one who, by God's gift, is able to care for us in our prayer - these are the markings embedded in our experience.

All of this is another way of saying we are beginning to sense in our bones the meaning of those words of the Council which first seemed so startling:

> Pastors must therefore realize that when the liturgy is celebrated something more is required than the mere observance of the laws governing valid and lawful celebration; it is also their duty to ensure that the faithful take part fully aware of what they are doing, actively engaged in the rite, and enriched by its effects (CSL #11 [DOL #11]).

"Something more is required"! An important vision of liturgical ministry lies behind these words and within our experience which increasingly bears them out. All liturgical ministers are "servants of the assembly" (EACW #37) who are to care for the people at the moment of that "holy exchange" spoken of earlier. But here, too, there is a shadow side to our experience - those times when we are not invited into keeping covenant with one another and God.

There are several challenges implied in this vision. First, liturgical ministries must be transformed from purely pragmatic functions into moments of ministry; liturgical ministers must be persons who are able to care for the people who gather at prayer. Second, they deserve to receive the kind of liturgical formation through catechesis and spiritual preparation which will enable them to be such caring persons (CSL #14 [DOL #14]).[6] Third, if caring for the people's prayer is their common concern and responsibility, we need to find ways to make their ministries a shared ministry.

TOWARDS A FULLER PROGRAM OF CARE

In the preceding sections we have lifted up some features of a vision of liturgy and liturgical ministry in order to ground and frame the central themes of catechesis, preparation, and evaluation which we have been reflecting on in the first part of this book. It only remains to suggest how these themes can be woven together in a program of liturgical care, reflecting both a program for the parish and the program of this book. While not an outline of a full-blown program of care, the suggestions are offered as characteristic features of our liturgical experience to date, as features we might well cultivate as we work toward such a program.

First, it seems timely to broaden our understanding of liturgical ministry from our narrower focus on the moment of celebration to include the kinds of ministry which now surround and support the liturgy. In addition to the ministers visible in the Sunday assembly, we need to include in our formation programs all those whose care prepares us and supports us in our prayer.

Second, our liturgical formation needs to include an integrated, step by step cycle of catechesis, preparation, and evaluative reflection. The cycle is initiated and shaped by a catechesis that is dialogic and attentive to our liturgical experience. It must provide a celebration that is able to catch us up in the "yes" of Jesus. And if the preparation is to be more than making educated guesses as to what is effective for our people, the cycle of care needs to be completed after the celebration by an evaluative reflection which leads us back into an earlier phase of the cycle, either catechesis or preparation.

Third, it will be obvious that our program should start with the catechesis and preparation of those who serve the assembly in roles of ministry and then expand in widening circles to the assembly. The rationale for this suggestion is based not on a sense of privilege due a ministerial elite, but rather on the critical impact their service has on the quality of the assembly's liturgical experience. "No other single factor affects the liturgy as much as the attitude, style, and bearing of the celebrant," write the U.S. bishops in their document, *Music in Catholic Worship* (#21). Members of the assembly cannot begin effective catechesis for the liturgy if they have not experienced good liturgy.

Fourth, and most importantly, we need to keep our ultimate pastoral aims clear: the paschal mystery which stands at the heart of the liturgy is meant to be lived out in our world with all its potential for death and new life. If our care for God's people at prayer is not to become comfortably narrow and self-serving, we need to constantly reaffirm the intrinsic connection between liturgy and social justice.[7] But that would be a topic for another book.

Finally, our understanding of the roles of catechesis, preparation, and evaluation must be broadened and deepened. It must include a catechesis which seeks to uncover the meaning the symbols and rituals have in the liturgical experience of the assembly. It must be broadened to include both a preparation and an evaluation which cares for the realization of that meaning in subsequent celebrations. The remainder of this book will be concerned with testing out how we might work out this kind of catechesis, preparation, and evaluation in a parochial setting.

Summary

1. The liturgy is the action of the entire assembly. The elements common to all liturgy - gathering, word, action, and sending - are built on an interplay of address and response. The exchange that takes place in the liturgy is a holy exchange between God and ourselves. The words and actions of the assembly embody the peak moment of that exchange, the event we call the paschal mystery. In the liturgy the assembly again voices, in remembrance and anticipation, the "yes" of Jesus which is at one and the same time God's "yes" to us and our "yes" to God.

2. Liturgical ministers include not only those who are called forth to speak and act in the name of Christ and of the assembly during the liturgy, but also those who prepare, catechize, and care for the liturgical life of the people outside the moments of actual celebration. Their common ministry is to enable the people to take part in the enduring liturgy of the Risen Lord. They are the servants of the assembly.

3. Catechesis, preparation, celebration, and evaluation can be woven into an integrated program of care for God's people at prayer. Such a program would begin with the liturgical ministers and widen out to the entire community. It should look beyond a narrow concern for the liturgy to the meaning the rites can have for the assembly as they live out their lives in a world in need of justice and peace.

Notes

1. Introductory reading on the experience and theological underpinnings of the new liturgy can be found in: James Dallen, *Gathering for Eucharist. A Theology of Sunday Assembly* (Old Hickory, TN: Pastoral Arts Associates of North America, 1982); Joseph Gelineau, *The Liturgy Today and Tomorrow* (New York: Paulist Press, 1978); Tad Guzie, *The Book of Sacramental Basics* (New York: Paulist Press, 1981); Mark Searle, *Liturgy Made Simple* (Collegeville: Liturgical Press, 1981).

2. "Whenever rites, according to their specific nature, make provision for communal celebration involving the presence and active participation of the faithful, it is to be stressed that this way of celebrating them is to be preferred, as far as possible, to a celebration that is individual and, so to speak, private."

3. "The Church earnestly desires that all the faithful be led to that full, conscious, and active participation in liturgical celebrations called for by the very nature of the liturgy. Such participation by the Christian people ... is their right and duty by reason of their baptism."

4. "In liturgical celebrations each one, minister or layperson, who has an office to perform, should do all of, but only, those parts which pertain to that office by the nature of the rite and the principles of liturgy."

5. For further reading on liturgical ministries, see: James B. Dunning, *Ministries: Sharing God's Gifts* (Winona, MN: St. Mary's Press, 1980); Robert W. Hovda, *Strong, Loving and Wise. Presiding in Liturgy* (Washington: Liturgical Conference, 1976); Robert W. Hovda, *There Are Different Ministries...* (Washington, D.C.: Liturgical Conference, 1975); and for an historical background, see: David N. Power, *Gifts That Differ. Lay Ministries Established and Unestablished* (New York: Pueblo, 1980).

6. "A prime need, therefore, is that attention be directed, first of all, to the liturgical formation of the clergy."

7. See, for example, the critique voiced by John J. Eagan, "Liturgy and Social Justice: An Unfinished Agenda," *Origins* 13 #15 (Sept. 22, 1983) 246–253 [later published by Liturgical Press as a pamphlet under the same title].

II
INVOLVING THE PARISH

Introduction

A word about the languages of liturgy

Two premises frame this part of the book. The first is the conviction that we need to be much more attentive to the non-verbal side of liturgy in caring for God's people at prayer. As a result of the Council's decision to allow us to return to a vernacular liturgy, we rediscovered that liturgy is to speak to us in ways that we understand, and we became enamored with words in our celebrations. We have only begun to recover our sense of balance about the critical role of the non-verbal ways in which the liturgy speaks to us. The second premise concerns our common assumption that the four component parts of the liturgy named earlier - gathering, word, action, and sending - are the basic building blocks with which we are to work in caring for the people's prayer. These four parts do indeed form the final pattern of liturgy, but they are woven together from yet more basic threads. Or, to change the image, these four parts are a chorus blending together the many voices in which liturgy speaks to us. It is to these voices of liturgy that we need to attend, to learn the ways liturgy speaks to us, and to nurture them in the assemblies for which we care.

If we ponder these four components further, we will discover that they each make use of four basic "liturgical languages": **space**, **time**, **action**, and **speech**. Speech and action are each prominent in the parts of the liturgy named after them, but they are also used in the other parts as well. For example, the liturgy of the word relies on actions as well as words, prayers accompany the sacramental actions, and the gathering and sending make use of both words and actions. The languages of space and time, however, often go unnoticed and uncared for. They, too, are to be found at work in each of the four parts of the liturgy and deserve more attention. For example, gathering and sending frame the liturgy and separate it from everyday life in the world. In the gathering we cross a boundary; we enter a time and place set apart. It is here, in a liturgical "time outside of time" and in a liturgical "place outside of place," that we are most prone to hear the word and sense the deed of a God who is beyond space and time. And in the sending we leave that "set apart" world and re-enter our everyday place and time. To be sure, liturgical time and space are not to be set in isolation from or opposition to our life in the everyday world, but they do introduce a pause or break into our everyday lives. It is these four languages that we wish to explore individually and in detail in this part of the book.

It is important to note that the word 'language' is being used analogously for these four ways in which liturgy speaks to and for us. When we hear the word 'language' we automatically think of using words, whether spoken or written, to communicate. Verbal language, then, provides the point of comparison for our analogy. Since we will not treat verbal language extensively until the final chapters, so as not to reduce the other "languages" to being mere frills tacked onto it, we need to start by reflecting on it briefly.

Verbal language is born for communication; its primary use is in conversation. Our speaking with one another is such an ordinary, everyday occurrence that we seldom stop to think about it. What happens in a conversation, if it is more than a monologue, seems simple enough. One person speaks, another listens. Then the hearer replies while the original speaker listens. The partners continue this switching of roles as long as the conversation lasts. And to what purpose? Their intent is to share an experience, a feeling, an understanding, a message. On closer inspection, we see that the exchange is simultaneously expression and communication. The speaker expresses what is within herself or himself - ideas, views, feelings, hopes - and that is communicated to the listener. Ever since the time of Aristotle these three key elements, speaker, hearer, and message, have been taken as the starting point for communications theory.

The process is actually more complex than that. Current communications theory, attentive to the fact that a process is taking place, has alerted us to three additional elements. The sender (speaker) encodes and transmits the message. The message is carried by some vehicle or channel of transmission. And the receiver (hearer) receives and decodes the message. In this schema we have: sender, encoding/sending, message, transmitting vehicle, receiving/decoding, and receiver. The message is safeguarded against distorting "noise" in the channel by repeated transmission, called redundancy, and by feedback to check out the accuracy. Language, in this schema, is the vehicle in which the message is encoded and through which the message is communicated.

Such analysis, unless we're careful, can lead us into thinking of language as a thing. Language is first and foremost something we use in conversing with one another. It is in the first instance a verb, not a noun. Language as a thing is no more than the precipitate of live communication. True, words can be written or electronically recorded to serve as a record of that event, or to allow us to communicate across barriers of time and space. Written and recorded language gives us a chance to retrieve and linger over what is said, to do an instant or slow-motion replay, to focus on particular aspects, to factor out subjective elements. But words can only capture a part of the whole range of what happens in live communication. We all know how much is lost when we cannot see the speaker's face or hear the tone of voice used. The difference between language as written or recorded words and as live speech is like that between script and play, rubric and ritual performance, recipe and cooking. In the end language must always be put back into its discourse-situation to have its full meaning. That is why many prefer to use the word 'speaking' rather than 'language' for the live event.

One final observation about verbal language. We use words to express and communicate what our views and feelings are, what people and things mean to us. We fashion language to give shape to our world and share that world with one another. But it is also true that language takes on an existence of its own, it is given to us. As we learn it, we are unconsciously taught how to see the world and everything and everyone in it, including ourselves. We and our world are shaped by our language. Language expresses and communicates a world of meaning, a meaning we both create and discover. It is an effective vehicle of communication only if those who use it inhabit a world of shared meaning.

We ordinarily do not think of space, time, and action as "languages," but if we stop and take a closer look at them, we'll find that they resemble spoken language in any number of ways. We use them as vehicles of communication. We encode many messages about our world in them in order to send those messages to others. We learn to read what they say, to decode the messages others have embedded in them for us. We shape them into symbol systems to bear these messages, but we and our world are also shaped by the messages embedded in the non-verbal systems we inherit. At the same time, each of these "languages" works in its own unique way. While there is much redundancy between them in what they communicate, each adds something unique to enrich the communication process.

The question remains, is it acceptable to speak of action, space, and time as "languages"? Study of human behavior in social psychology has drawn the parallel in the area of bodily action and accustomed us to think of it as "body language." Space and time, however, seem to present a different case. Are they not things in themselves, nothing more than the arena for speech and action? But even there space and time are measured by what we do and say in them; they are a dimension of our saying and doing. In a real sense we evoke and experience them as human space and human time; we subtly shape them to sustain and further our acting and speaking; we invest them with meaning. We can rightly speak of them, though analogously, as "languages."

Space, time, action, and speech are the four human languages taken up into the liturgy to be our language of prayer. They are the "languages" on which liturgy is built.

A word about this part

In the chapters that follow we will explore these four languages in detail. Two chapters, one more general and one more specific, will be devoted to each language. Each chapter will follow the same pattern. We will begin with a descriptive essay on our experience of the language in question, to make us aware of what we do so naturally and unconsciously as we use these languages in everyday life and in liturgy. We will then explore how we might go about doing a catechesis of that language, using the three steps of attending, reflecting, and applying developed earlier. Finally, we will draw some brief implications from what we have learned for our work of preparing and evaluating the liturgical celebrations of our people.

Before we begin, a few words about how to use the chapters in this part are appropriate. First, you will likely note that the reflective essay at the beginning of each chapter anticipates step two of the three-step catechetical method we are exploring in this book. The written character of a book suggested this reversal. In a live setting we would have been able to reflect on the liturgical languages together after we had become attentive to our experience of them. We can, however, preserve something of that live exploration if you read the essay sections in a mood of reminiscence and reverie. Take the essays as an invitation to daydream about your own experience, to substitute what you discover there for what I say. Second, in envisioning how you might use this book in working with the people you serve, please hold to the process adamantly. Have them attend to their own experience as the starting point. The essays in this book are not meant to be used as a "reading assignment" given out ahead of time; they are meant to help you reflect on your own experience, so that you in turn can help your people reflect on theirs. My fondest hope will be realized if you find these chapters helpful in developing your own style of catechesis for the liturgy, and then decide to set the book aside.

1

Liturgical Space

LITURGICAL SPACE IS THE FIRST LANGUAGE WE WILL TAKE UP.
It is one of the most basic of our liturgical languages, for it
subtly determines, for good or for ill, the possibilities and limits of
what can happen in the assembly. This chapter will take a
general, structural approach to liturgical space.

THE EXPERIENCE OF LITURGICAL SPACE

What is space?[1] We use the word in many ways. "We need more
space" - physical or psychological. "There is a lot of empty space
that needs to be filled." "I love the wide open spaces of the plains."
"Outer space is vast and unlimited." Space stands for room, for
distance, for volume. We tend to think of it as an empty
container, something to be filled by people or things. In its
bedrock meaning, space is vast and unlimited, it is as yet
undifferentiated by anything within it.

But once we have begun to fill it with objects, with ourselves,
space takes on a different character. It becomes place. "Put
everything in its place." "Go to your place." "There's no place for
me." "They placed him at the scene of the crime." "They found a
place of their own." "She's a displaced person." "That is our home
place." Place is space with a border drawn round it, filled with a
single person or object, or with many people and objects whose
relative distances can be measured or traversed. Place is specific,
occupied, limited space.

How does space become human place? It all starts with our
bodies. Our bodies locate us in space. The space our bodies fill is

our place. We are here, not there. Our bodies limit us to the place where we are. But they also give us a way to connect with the space around us. We notice people and objects around us and place them in relation to ourselves. By moving about in space we can claim another "there" as our "here." Our bodies center the world for us, we experience them as the point from which we orient ourselves in space, by which we organize the surrounding space and claim it as our own. That, incidentally, is in part why falling in love is such a powerful experience. Our world is no longer centered on ourselves, but on an embodied other. More about our organization of space in a moment.

Our bodies not only center space for us, they also orient us in space and provide us with our sense of direction. The position of our upright body measures up and down, right and left, ahead and behind. These bodily orientations quickly move beyond their purely spatial meanings, however, and take on human meaning and value. Up and down serve to describe what is superior and inferior, or heady and solidly grounded. Right and left are associated with what is benevolent and sinister, or unimaginative and artistic. Front and back come to mean what lies in the future and in the past, or the self which is seen, to be presented with dignity ("face"), and unseen, to be protected or hidden in shame ("behind").

The potential space has for bearing meaning for us begins to emerge more fully as we organize and humanize it through our human activity. All our bodily senses have a part to play.[2] We identify particular places through sight, hearing, smell, and touch. We need only recall how acute any one of these senses becomes when a person's other senses are impaired.

For the majority of us it is sight that plays the most basic role. When we look around us, our eyes ceaselessly scan our visual field to identify what is of interest or familiar to us. It may be a prominent feature of a landscape, familiar faces in a crowd of people, or highlights of color and light in a painting. Our eyes focus on these features, and all else blends into a single, unnoticed background that we are often hard pressed to describe with any degree of accuracy or detail. At its farthest reach that background stretches to a horizon which marks the boundary of our vision. The objects and people within that bounded area are connected to us by lines of sight as well as by the paths we might take to reach them, and we visually interconnect them with one another. We soon know favorite things and familiar faces on sight. It is not coincidental that so many of our words of knowing are really words of seeing.

Along with our bodily senses, our bodily actions have much to do with claiming space as our place.[3] Of all those actions, movement in most important, for we can make any portion of space our own by simply moving into it. We stake out space for ourselves by walking around it and by filling it with our bodies through the practical movements we trace there each day as well as through the movements we trace in the exuberance of a dance. If our movements were colored threads, it would be marvelous to see what an intricate pattern of places we weave together as we move through each day.

The movement we're speaking of here is not just random movement, that normally leaves us lost and without a sense of the space around us. Nor is it the cowed, deferential kind of movement we often see in public places, someone passing through with head bowed, shoulders curled forward, hands and arms tucked in. That clearly tells any observer "I'm not trying to invade your territory; I don't consider this my place." Rather, it is, in the broadest sense of that word, a purposeful kind of movement that makes us feel at home where we are.

Nor is the movement of which we're speaking restricted to locomotion. We also make space our place through what we do in it. There are many kinds of bodily activities we perform day by day wherever we are. The more humanly significant they are, the more apt we are to set aside a special place for their performance.

The family home is an apt illustration of this. Walls separate and secure the family space from the outside world. There are rooms for eating, sleeping, relaxing, entertaining, bathing, and doing work of various sorts. Each is decorated and appointed according to the activity carried on there. The rooms' interior arrangement, location, and connecting doorways and passages tell us much about how important those activities are, who does them, and how public or intimate they are to the family and its members. We can take this one step further. How we shape the family space also reveals the structured relationships within the family. It tells us how we fit together. Think, for example, of the seating arrangements around the family table and what they tell us about how each of us fits into the family.

The family home is so important to us because of what happens there, the events that bind us, the nurture given, the leisure shared, the love exchanged. And we enshrine its value in our memory, to be revisited again and again long after we have left the physical place behind. Similar things can be said about neighborhoods, cities, nations. But few other places bear the same sense of meaning and value for us as the family home.[4]

The places we construct and hallow by what we do there are not the only significant places. There are others that are "found," that are given to us. Their significance may stem from an event that happened to occur there, a famous battle, a moment of self-discovery in solitude, a proposal of marriage. We are wont to enshrine these places, too, whether in memory or with the historical markers that adorn our roadsides and famous buildings. We visit these shrines again and again, as long as they continue to exist and the value they safeguard for us remains real.

One final word before we move on to liturgical space. Human places are those portions of space, including our own body-place, which we come to know and value by our being there and acting there. Whether we find them or shape them, we incorporate them into a world that tells us who we are and what we value. And so, in the end, by continuing to dwell and work in those places, we are shaped by them - by the story they tell us and by the values they teach us.

What, then, is liturgical space? It is the holy place where the assembly gathers together, listens to the word of God, enacts a covenantal action, and is sent back into the world. In some rare cases the place may have become a gathering place because of God's past deed there. Such is the case with churches built in the land of Jesus to mark events in his life, so that we might gather there to remember. More often, though, a site is selected, a gathering place is erected, and it becomes a holy place by what we do there.

Here, too, it all starts with the body. Like human space, liturgical space is centered by the body of believers who gather there; it is hallowed and given abiding value by the holy rites we do there. It is our being there together, our shared activity, that makes space a worship place. If this suggests a certain arbitrariness about our gathering places, well and good. Jesus taught that his Abba is to be worshiped everywhere, in spirit and truth. It is first his human body, and then the body that is his church, that we believe to be the dwelling place of God. Our history shows that we have gathered in many places to celebrate liturgy, in the homes of early christians, at a river bank for baptism, in Jewish and pagan temples, in the roman multi-purpose halls called basilicas, in hidden corners or jail cells in times of persecution, and in an Iowa cornfield for a papal visit, as well as in the whole splendid array of church buildings built over the centuries.

This has important consequences for how we think about liturgical space. Our christian understanding does not start with a physical place, a building called church. We start with the assembly. The assembly is the church, the temple of God. Liturgical space is wherever the church gathers to pray and keep covenant. Liturgy is our action, not a stage performance that can only be given for spectators in a particular kind of building. The ancient christian name for the physical gathering place is not "church," but rather "the house of the church." It is like the family home.

Having said all that, we need to acknowledge that it is the most natural thing in the world for us to set aside a special gathering place for the holy action we call liturgy. And when we do that, we follow the patterns we use in establishing any human place. We mark its boundaries with walls and processions, to distinguish inside and outside. We set aside places for two groups of people who play a critical role in the celebration, the assembly at large and its ministers. We reserve areas within the structure for the important actions that happen there and focus those areas, visually and spatially, on central symbolic objects like ambo, table, and font. We even use bodily orientations to lend importance and dignity - placing persons and objects higher, in front, to the presider's right. It takes only a little attentive observation of such arrangements, or a simple tracing of the movements of members of the assembly, to see that our relationships are encoded in the liturgical space as surely as a family's relationships are encoded in the space of a family home.

Liturgical space, like human place, is something we shape to express and communicate our values, our relationships, our world. In the end, as with human space, our assembly place also shapes us and our world. It determines the possibilities and limits of how we can be together and act together. Unnoticed and often uncared for, it is one of the most critical liturgical languages we use to tell ourselves who we are and what our world is like.

And what message does this "house of the church" convey to us through its liturgical space? Place where we are reborn, it roots our sense of belonging. Place of gathering Sunday after Sunday, it gives us a sense of continuity, pattern, and connectedness in our lives. Shaped to house a people, it tells us that we are a people and how we are to relate to one another and serve each other. Place of story-telling and ritual-making, it keeps the memory and deed of Jesus alive in our hearts and lives. Replica and miniature of our world and all its human places, it can model the meaning of life in that world. In sum, our liturgical space has the power to anchor and map our human world and our christian journey through it.

Against the background of this descriptive essay, let us now take a look at the catechesis of liturgical space.

CATECHESIS FOR LITURGY

Attending. A liturgical catechesis oriented to adult learning begins by having us attend to our experience. In this first phase, the educational task is to recover, describe, and name our actual experience of liturgical space in the celebration of liturgy.

How can we recover our experience of liturgical space, given its subtle and unnoticed quality? Let me suggest two ways, the first based on reminiscing and the other on isolating and re-creating the experience.

The reminiscing can begin when the study group has gathered and been put into a reflective mood. It starts with a return, in memory, to some special place. There are in each of our lives places that are very dear to us, places that have a strong hold on us. The family home, whether of childhood days or later years, is one. It is an excellent starting point because it is so common to all of us. We each have other such personal places as well. Having each one choose a favorite personal place is a second option. The local parish church provides a third option. It serves well as the final place to reminisce about, if several are used, because it brings us to an explicitly liturgical space.

Once we have journeyed there in memory, we need to linger there in memory and imagination, recovering the sensory details of that space, its size, shape, layout, texture, colors, smells, and sights. We need to remember and relive the things that happened there. We need to see, in our memory's eye, the persons who were there and what they did. It is easy to develop questions for someone to use in leading the group through this reminiscing.

When we have recovered the experience of that place, we are ready, first individually and then together in groupings of a size that encourages exchange, to describe and name that experience. Again, questions can be easily devised to accomplish this; they might even be incorporated into the reminiscing process itself. Descriptive questions will be concerned with recording sensory impressions, with recounting events that happened there, with naming people who were there. It is important to attend to these externals of the experience, as noted in chapter one, lest we allow the "sacramental sign" dimension of the liturgy to evaporate into thin air. Naming questions will seek to surface the inner human quality of those experiences, the feelings, emotions, hopes, and dreams they evoked in us. Putting the outer and inner dimensions into words for ourselves and others leaves us ready for the second phase.

The second way of recovering our experience of space is by visiting several varied spaces. The field trip, done together or at each one's leisure in advance of the learning session, should include both liturgical and non-liturgical spaces. Most cities of any size offer a variety of intriguing non-liturgical spaces, including shopping malls, open-air plazas, hotel lobbies and foyers, parks with hidden corners, and neighborhoods with a special atmosphere. This technique is more fruitful if several varied spaces are visited. Contrasts highlight and clarify our experiences.

What is to be done when we are on site? The first thing to do is to roam around in the space, to take in its sights, smells, colors, textures, and to just get the feel of the space by moving about in it. It is important to remain in each place and to attend to it with our bodily senses until we experience its impact. This cannot be rushed.

Once the place has made an impact on us, we can turn our attention to describing and naming the experience. I recommend that we go on the field trip equipped with three questions to ask ourselves once we have felt the impact of the place. First, a descriptive question: what strikes me most about this place? Second, a naming question: what feelings does it evoke in me? And third, an application question: if I were to pray here, what would my prayer be? If I were to plan a liturgy for this space, what would it be like? It helps greatly to jot down our answers to these questions on the spot, lest we forget our impressions or edit them in our memory. The third question has been included for that reason, though it anticipates the third phase of the catechetical process.

Enlightened by the insights gained from these experiences, we are then ready to gather in group session, first to report on our visits and our answers to the first two questions, and then, as in the approach based on reminiscing, to begin the second phase of reflecting together on what the experience means.

Reflecting. The second phase of liturgical catechesis is reflecting on the experience we have recovered, whether by reminiscing or by visiting. The educational task is to learn what that experience means for us and what it has meant for others. In this phase we need to do two things, to glean the meaning our experience has and, with the help of a resource person, to set that alongside the meaning to be found in the larger story of our people's past experience.

Gathering up the meaning the experience of space has for us can begin as an individual activity. But I am convinced it is best done together, and at some point it must become a shared activity if we are to arrive at the larger sense of a shared journey proper to a church that calls itself a people. For what happens in this phase is the weaving together of fragmentary experiences into a world of meaning, into themes that trace their way through a life story.

Again, it is not that difficult to formulate questions to gently lead the group in this gathering up of meaning. What have places like home, or our special places, told us about ourselves, about the place others have in our lives, about the things we value together, about the shape of our lives and our world? What continuing role do those places play? Do they continue to shape us? Do we use them to remember what is important to us? Do we change and alter them, or discard them, as our life story grows and unfolds? Are there places that continually draw us back, particularly in times of confusion or decision? And perhaps the most important question of all is the follow-up question that must be posed for every answer to these questions: Why? What specific features of those places give them the power to speak in these ways? This "why?" is critical because it forces us to see how our humanized space concretely encodes these meanings and messages.

Let me add an observation as a brief interlude here. So far in this reflective gathering up of meaning we have focused on our experience of human space. Starting there and moving on to our experience of liturgical space is a good catechetical method; it follows the very make-up of our liturgical rites. They are symbolic human actions taken up into a world of religious meaning. Drawing out the meaning of those underlying human symbols is an effective way to shed light on the meaning of their liturgical counterparts.

When we turn to our experience of liturgical space to gather up its meaning, those same questions stand us in good stead. What does the assembly place tell us about God, about ourselves, about our life journey as God's people? How do we shape and reshape our liturgical space as we grow as God's people, and how does it shape us? These questions can be phrased graphically in terms of our gathering for sacramental and Sunday celebrations. Here, as with our human places, the follow-up question is always the critical one: Why? Only in seeking to answer that question do we connect what the liturgy tells us and accomplishes in us with the concrete symbols and symbolic languages that are the sacramental sign.

It is at this point, having reflected on what our collective experience means to us, that we need to turn to a resource person for the matching information from our larger history and experience. It is not my purpose here to provide the actual input; I only wish to indicate some themes and resources that might be drawn upon.

First, the scriptures remain the staple resource. A number of themes found there might be of help: Jesus' words to the Samaritan woman, in John 4, about the approaching time when God will be worshiped in spirit and truth, and not in any exclusive place; his use of the temple theme in reference to his own body; Paul's thought on the church as the body of Christ and the temple of the Spirit; the mystery of Jesus' humanity as the place of God's presence among us, especially as developed in John. Similarly, the scriptures present an enlightening array of places which the early disciples used for prayer, word, and sacrament: the temple, synagogues, their homes, a supper room, a pool by the roadside, a jail cell in Rome, to name a few.

Second, our past history tells a richly varied story of how we have adapted and shaped spaces for our liturgy. Line drawings of church shapes and their interior arrangements across the ages, coupled with an account of how those designs embodied deep-seated understandings of relationships of assembly to God, of assembly to its ministers, of assembly to the surrounding world, have an enormous power to unlock our tradition to us. Any number of works published recently provide all the help a resource person will need in putting together a historical sketch.[5]

Third, the U.S. bishops' document, *Environment and Art in Catholic Worship*, especially part three (#39–54), offers many fine insights on the kind of meaning we are to seek in contemporary design for liturgical space.

Fourth, the local community may well know of or have within its midst people who are architects, interior designers, or environmental artists. Social psychologists who work in a field called "proxemics" can also help us sort out how spatial arrangements mirror social structures. Persons such as these represent a resource that we may want to tap on occasion.

It helps to be clear about what kind of input we want from such resource persons. Obviously, detailed history and intricate theory are not our primary need. What we need is a larger perspective that will help us situate our own experience within that of the tradition out of which we live. As that healthy interplay reaches fruition, we are ready to move on to the final phase of liturgical catechesis.

Applying. The task of the third phase of liturgical catechesis is to help us apply what we have learned to our continued celebration of the liturgy.

A first application follows naturally. Those who have reflected on their experience of liturgical space will normally discover within themselves a deeper sensitivity and susceptibility to what it can say to them. A brief wrap-up discussion can help them articulate this for themselves and make their own resolutions about how they will participate in the liturgy.

A second application falls to those who prepare and evaluate the liturgy. That will be the concern of the next section.

PREPARATION AND EVALUATION

In preparing the liturgy week after week we normally work with an inherited liturgical space that is already shaped and fully appointed. Only rarely do we have the opportunity to design a totally new space or make extensive renovations to an existing one. These latter situations call for a more extended process of study and reflection than we have described above. The simpler kind of catechesis outlined above is adequate for our normal preparation process and flows into it naturally.

Caring for the meaning liturgical space has for an assembly requires taking into account the actual place where the people assemble for the liturgy. Committee members need to have a feel for their space, its limits and possibilities. It is important for them and the ministers appointed for the celebration to walk around in that space as they prepare for the liturgy. An on-site meeting to discuss how to fit the liturgy to the space can be of great help as they do the preparations, particularly when special occasions call for a fresh use of the space to highlight some facet of the celebration. An idea that sounds great or terrible over the meeting table may appear in a different light in a walk-through in the actual space. The key thing for the committee is to see the space from the assembly's perspective. They will want to pay close attention to the values and memories the assembly already associates or can associate with the space and to the assembly's line of sight and relationship to movement, whether as participants or viewers. Sight and movement provide the basic starting point for how the assembly orders its gathering place into a symbol of its faith world.

A brief word about resources for preparing liturgical space: there are many pastoral aids available for studying and readying liturgical space.[6] Environmental and performing artists can also be consulted. Our basic resource, however, should be our own experience. Periodically visiting other churches and re-visiting our own to reflect on the space and let it resonate with us, as suggested above, ensure that our work will be rooted in our own experience in a way no other resource can. That, finally, is our aim - to prepare a liturgy which speaks to the spiritual needs of our local assembly in a familiar language, including that of the place that houses them.

What qualities ought we look for as we prepare and evaluate our use of liturgical space in liturgy? In addition to the general norms and qualities laid out in the chapter on qualities and criteria, the following are particularly pertinent to our overall design of liturgical space.

Norm: "The norm for designing liturgical space is the assembly and its liturgies" (EACW #42). The design should be tailored to the particular liturgy to be celebrated. It should also reflect the community to be assembled for the celebration.

Prepare and evaluate:

1. *The assembly's space.* In good pastoral liturgy the liturgical space is the assembly's place, designed so that it "clearly invites and needs an assembly of people to complete it," "brings the people close together so that they can see and hear the entire liturgical action," and "helps them feel involved and become involved" (EACW #24). Good liturgical space communicates "a sense of being the gathering place of the initiated community" (EACW #53). It reflects their human diversity and spiritual journeys. It takes special account of the deprived and handicapped in the assembly's midst, since they are most directly affected by the physical and human accessibility of the place. It does not dominate the assembly or replace it as the primary liturgical symbol (EACW #28, 30, 39, 41). Evaluation question: Was the space truly the assembly's gathering place?

2. *A hospitable climate.* "Liturgy flourishes in a climate of hospitality" (EACW #11) marked by human warmth and welcome. Good liturgical space invites people into the liturgy without coercion. It gathers them without dominating them. It does not pretend it is more important than the word they hear and the deed they do there. It tells them that the ancient rite is theirs to do in a world of today (EACW #11, 33, 35, 52). Was the space hospitable?

3. *A holy climate.* The "liturgy's climate is one of awe, mystery, wonder, reverence, thanksgiving and praise" (EACW #34). Good liturgical space invites people to experience the presence of the Holy One in their lives and conveys the feeling of wholeness and healing that comes from being God's own. It is above all the simple, cared for beauty of the assembly place that bears for us this sense of the holy (EACW #12, 24). Was the space holy?

4. *A serving space.* Good liturgical space serves the assembly and its ministers without interrupting the celebration or proclaiming itself or its creator (EACW #24-25, 37). Did the space serve the assembly?

5. *A simple space.* Liturgical space strives for a simple and attractive beauty that invites worshipers to experience the God beyond. It seeks a simplicity that disavows sinful human pretense and refuses to hold a pilgrim people hostage to a single time and place (EACW #12, 36, 41). Is the gathering place kept appropriately simple?

6. *A flexible space.* Good liturgical practice in an age of pluralism and change looks for a flexible liturgical space that is open to the needs of diverse assemblies and to local adaptation of the liturgy. It also allows for other pastorally responsible uses of the space (EACW #39). Is the gathering space kept appropriately flexible?

7. *A witnessing place.* Worshiping communities belong to a broader human community and a larger world to which they are called to give witness and service in their use and appointment of liturgical space (EACW #38-39). Liturgical space can never afford to ignore the larger human space of which it is a part or the larger human family from which it gathers the assembly. What does the liturgical space witness to the world?

Summary question: Did the assembling place give meaning to the lives of those assembled and express their human and spiritual journeys?

Notes

1. In developing the materials for this section I have depended heavily on: Edmond Barbotin, "Human Space," in his *The Humanity of Man*, translated by Matthew J. O'Connell (Maryknoll: Orbis Books, 1975), 29-90; Yi-Fu Tuan, *Space and Place. The Perspective of Experience* (Minneapolis: University of Minnesota Press, 1977); and, to a lesser extent, Arthur A. Vogel, "Body-Meaning," in his *Body Theology. God's Presence in Man's World* (New York: Harper & Row, 1973), 87-110. The reflective writing style of Barbotin has served as a model for me in the descriptive essays in this and subsequent chapters.

2. The next chapter will focus on the sensory experience of space, especially visual experience.

3. Bodily action, especially movement, will be the focus of chapter five, below.

4. In using this example of the family home we should also acknowledge that the mobility of many families may undermine the role a home has in shaping values and identity.

5. See, for example: Peter G. Cobb, "The Architectural Setting of the Liturgy," in Cheslyn Jones, Geoffrey Wainwright, Edward Yarnold (ed.), *The Study of the Liturgy* (New York: Oxford Univ. Press, 1978), 473–487; Pierre Jounel, "Places of Christian Assembly: The First Millennium," in The Bishops' Committee on the Liturgy and The Catholic University of America Center for Pastoral Liturgy, *The Environment for Worship. A Reader* (Washington, D.C.: USCC Publications, 1980), 15–27; Robert E. Webber, "Worship and Space," in his *Worship Old and New* (Grand Rapids: Zondervan, 1982), 151–160; James F. White, "The Language of Space," in his *Introduction to Christian Worship* (Nashville: Abingdon, 1980), 76–109.

6. For example: Gabe Huck, *Liturgy with Style and Grace* (Chicago: Liturgy Training Publications, 1984), 28–33; Gabe Huck (ed.), *Simple Gifts. A Collection of Ideas and Rites from Liturgy*, vol. I (Washington, D.C.: The Liturgical Conference, 1974), 3–31; John Mossi (ed.), *Modern Liturgy Handbook. A Study and Planning Guide for Worship* (New York: Paulist Press, 1976), 91–125; Thomas G. Simmons, *The Ministry of Liturgical Environment* (Collegeville: Liturgical Press, 1984).

2

Liturgical Environment

WE HAVE LOOKED AT LITURGICAL SPACE IN AN OVERALL, STRUC-
tural sort of way. This chapter will focus in on the specific,
changeable ways in which that space is shaped into a liturgical
environment. A certain amount of overlap between this and the
previous chapter has proved unavoidable.

THE EXPERIENCE OF LITURGICAL ENVIRONMENT

How can we begin to understand what the liturgical environment is and how it affects us?[1] Let me start with a question which
my continuing experience poses for me.

When I do parish workshops on the way liturgy speaks to us I
often begin with a bit of "before and after" discussion. When
asked to name what they remember most deeply and fondly
about the old liturgy, people invariably name the use of Latin, a
sense of mystery and awe, and a whole list of things like purple
statue coverings, incense, bells and clappers, processions, the
sound of the chant, and the communion fast. When asked to
name what strikes them most about the new liturgy, they
typically single out the use of a vernacular which they fully
understand, a diminished sense of awe and mystery, a sense of
the liturgy being "ours," and a whole host of things like the sign
of peace and the various roles which special ministers exercise.

Hearing these same answers over and over has convinced me
more and more that the old liturgy spoke primarily through
sensory experience. It relied heavily on the engaging of our bodily

senses, rather than on words spoken in a familiar tongue, to convey the sense of God's presence and holiness. The liturgical renewal has restored a great many prized values to our celebrations - a greater simplicity, an understandable language, and especially the assembly's sense of mutual involvement and service. But the answers people give raise a question. Has the new liturgy failed to embody those values sufficiently? Has it lost the deep kind of bodily involvement we felt in the older liturgy? Is that, perhaps, why so many feel we have lost a sense of holiness and mystery in our celebrations? Has the restoration of the vernacular led us to rely too heavily on words which carry a clear and understandable message and not enough on bodily actions and an environment which appeals to the bodily senses and thus captures our imagination and spirits?

When we hold a human celebration it is the most natural thing in the world to create an environment for it. We are not content to gather in a space that feels like a vacuum, or a building that is an empty shell. When we look for a place in which to make a permanent home, we do not settle for bland motel rooms that look like every motel room we have ever occupied. In both cases we decorate that space and surround ourselves with a wide array of objects, sights, and sounds to create an atmosphere that engages us totally, in body, mind, and spirit. That is the kind of human experience we need to explore as we reflect on liturgical environment.

How do we go about creating a human environment?

Perhaps the words 'decorate' and 'redecorate' say it best. Whether it is a place we'll only use briefly for a party or a place where we intend to dwell, we change our surroundings to our liking. For a party we may simply add streamers, hangings, flowers, and other appropriate decorations and furnishings to ready the place. Setting up house is a more dramatic example. We often start by recovering the surfaces of the place with paint, rugs, fabrics, drapery. We choose and blend their colors to match our taste. We install the kind of lighting we like, romantic here, practical there. We add plants. We arrange furniture with great care. We provide a music system for our enjoyment. We create special areas with different moods - a cozy, nest-like area for reading, a bright area for working, an open, inviting area for entertaining, a secluded area for familiar and intimate times. We surround those areas with favorite objects. And to put the finishing touch on it all we display our favorite knick-knacks and keepsakes and hang our favorite pictures, especially those of family and friends.

If we look at that experience closely, we see that the environment thus created is a complex overlay of various sensory spaces. The visual space is the most dominant. Light and dark areas, contrasting and complementary shapes, patterns, and colors, various objects to be seen, seating arrangements and other identifiable areas, all these combine to create a visual space filled with select objects and made vivid to the eye by the quality and shades of light and color.

But there are other sensory spaces as well. Surface textures and objects create an intimate world which we love to touch and which we can identify by feel, even in the dark. The music we play surrounds us and wraps us in quadrophonic sound. Flowers, furniture polish, air fresheners, and spice pomanders mark various areas with their scents. We thus transform our environment into a rich array of tactile, auditory, and olfactory spaces to complement the visual space.

In a remarkable interplay these spaces each add something special to our experience of our environment. Sight and sound each evoke their own experience of distance. We see stereoscopically, in three dimensions, and judge distances by converging lines and the relative size of things. Hearing uses loudness and fading sound as cues to determine distance. Heavy odors, a big sound, and the feel of an object or of a warm bath each suggest volume in their own ways. Freighted with its unique sensations and the memories it evokes, each sensory space enhances and enriches the others. That is why we can use them as metaphors of each other. We speak of flat and sharp tastes, of heavy and light odors, of loud and quiet colors, of bright and dull sounds, or of rough and smooth sounds. But in the end, visual space, along with bodily movement, remains our dominant way of sensing space.

One more factor needs to be added at this point. We set aside private places and shape their sensory environment to please our personal taste, and those places tell us much about ourselves. But we also shape public places in the same way, and those places become a form of public communication. Return, for a moment, to the experience of redecorating we were reflecting on. Notice how the redecoration is something we do through our bodily activity and the use of materials. But we leave more than the physical imprint of our hand on our surroundings; we leave the imprint of our personality as well. Notice, too, how often the environments we create have an invitational quality. Subdued, romantic light invites intimacy. Winding stairways call for dramatic entrances. Pictures and keepsakes encourage inspection and comment. Open space invites people to move about and fill it and to watch each other. Easy chairs placed side by side in a secluded nook encourage personal sharing; larger seating arrangements encourage public conversations. In all this are we not shaping our sensory environment to do two things, to present ourselves to others and to welcome them into our lives? We shape our environment to be a place of bodily interaction with others.

Each sensory dimension woven into a public environment discloses and invites in its own way. Sight remains basic. But what we see are not just the objects, colors, and such that surround us, but each other. We watch one another to decipher all the postures, movements, and facial expressions that reveal what we are thinking and feeling. And ultimately, it is the gaze and touch that fulfill all that our environment has promised. For in the gaze we see something more than mere objects. We do not just look at another human being as an object of sight, but as one like ourselves who sees, who is subject, who is person. Though the eyes can see things at a great distance, it is only when we are within a few feet of each other that we can truly gaze on the face of another to read what is written there. The sight of a friend from afar compels us to draw near, within the touch of each other's gaze. From there it is only a short distance to the touch of the hand that draws us as near to another human as we can be. That is the goal of our environment-making, to humanize our place, to make it a place where we can meet and be human together.

How do we create a liturgical environment?

It often begins, once we have found a gathering place, with a process much like that of our home-redecorating, but on a grander scale, since the gathering is larger.

Think back, for a moment, to your parish church or favorite worship place. Wander around it in your imagination with senses alert. What have we done there to create an environment of prayer? We fill the place with light and darkness, we filter the sunlight through stained glass, we direct and focus artificial light, we break the darkness with flickering candles and vigil lamps. Why? To guide our eyes to what is important. We add color in myriad ways, with paint and hangings, with mosaics and stained glass, with flowers and vestments. Why? Again, to attract the eye and set a mood. We enthrone statues and holy keepsakes to visually tell a holy story. We burn incense and anoint with scented oil to tell of offered prayers and offered lives. We provide platforms, lofts, and amplifying systems so that speakers and singers may be seen and heard. We locate table, lectern, and font at the visual focal points of what we do together. We arrange chairs for ministers and assembly so that our gaze may include each other as together we behold the signs of God's presence.

Notice what a prominent part the senses play here, as in our human decorating. The liturgical environment is a complex overlay of many sensory spaces, visual, auditory, olfactory, tactile. Each speaks to us in its unique way, to tell some facet of our story, and all are meant to enrich each other. As in the case of human environment, we would expect visual space to remain our predominant way of experiencing our liturgical surroundings.[2]

But if we're honest about our experience of a liturgical environment, we also know that its various sensory spaces can be at odds with each other, especially because of the scale of the gathering. For example, we use an intimate voice only with someone nearby; we use a public voice for larger groups in a larger space. Similarly, eyes and facial expression communicate well within shorter distances, but only minimally at greater distances. Loudspeakers enable us to amplify an intimate tone of voice and auditory space to reach hundreds of people seated in a large visual space that impedes communicating by facial expression and would normally demand a public voice. Or again, informal gestures which seem natural in a small gathering appear distracting in a large assembly. Timid colors may fail to focus the attention of such an assembly and timid sounds may fail to surround them in an aural embrace. Or colors, tones, sounds, and gestures that are too large and bold may overpower and violate a small gathering place.

What the last paragraph suggests is that liturgical environment, like the environment of public human places, is meant for and measured by the people who gather there. It is a complex sensory language of disclosure and invitation through which an embodied people speak to one another of who they are and who they are to become as God's people. Light and color, shapes and textures bespeak a welcome, a mood, a common point of attention. A handsome book enthroned on an ambo and then in human hands speaks of a word that is as precious to us as dew or as powerful as a sword. What then, we might ask, does a throw-away pamphlet printed on newsprint say about God's word? A table simply set and placed so that all may gather to eat tells of the companioning and nurturing needed for the journey ahead. A seating arrangement which allows all in the assembly, whether member or minister, to be physically bonded by gaze and touch as they listen to God's word and break a blessed bread begs for mutuality, reconciliation, and full inclusion of all.

What the liturgical environment tells us, then, is that we are a people, a people summoned by God's word, nourished by the grain of wheat that fell into the ground, and sent to invite a world into a kingdom. It tells the story of our journey as disciples, how we met the Lord Jesus on the way and were sent to tell the others. Its manner of telling is not that of audible words which chronicle beliefs and deeds, but rather that of the subtle voices known only to the other senses, voices which lead us to feel in our bones what it means to be God's people. We decorate and shape the environment of our gathering place to embody that message in full sensory fashion, and the environment in turn shapes us.

I began this essay on the experience of liturgical environment with a question posed by people's reflections on the old and new liturgy. Is the new liturgy too easily satisfied with communicating meaning and values through words and too little concerned with embodying in sensory forms what the rites have to say? People's experience urges us to admit that this is so. Our collected folk wisdom puts it very graphically: "one picture is better than a thousand words"; or again, "if I hear it, I forget it; if I see it, I remember it; if I do it, I know it." We are whole beings, made up of body and spirit. The way to our spirit is through our body. This is true of human interaction, and it is also true of God's way of approaching us. The symbolic rites and languages of liturgy follow this precise route. They touch our spirits by first touching our bodies. Speaking and hearing words is one channel of communication. But so are seeing, touching, smelling, and moving about. And they have the advantage of not being as shop-worn and trivial as the words which constantly bombard us in our world. They are able to evoke a whole range of human feelings and responses which words cannot. It is for that reason that we need to learn more about the way in which the liturgical environments we create express and shape the meaning the liturgy has for us.

CATECHESIS FOR LITURGY

Attending. The first catechetical task is to attend to our actual experience of our liturgical environment and ask ourselves what we actually experience at the liturgy. In the method we are following, that involves recovering, describing, and naming the experience.

The first technique we can use to help adult learners recover that experience is reminiscing on it. Let me name several ways in which this might be done.

One way is to engage the group in the type of "before and after" discussion mentioned at the beginning of this chapter. People find it easy to relive their experiences of the old liturgy together, so this reminiscing can be done as a group process. An easy starting question is "what do you remember most about the liturgy before the changes?" Christmas, with its heavy sensory overlay, can serve as an alternate topic in groups of people who have had no experience of the old liturgy. It is important that we take the time to first describe our impressions before trying to interpret them, lest we miss the very things that form the sensory languages.

A second way is to reminisce first about our family home and then about our parish church. When the group is in a reflective mood, we can begin by going back in memory and imagination to those places. Because of the strength of our memories and associations with its surroundings, the family home can serve as a powerful example to first sort out the different sensory spaces. Turning then to the parish church we can build on that awareness in an explicitly liturgical context. Again, the lead questions need to focus first on the physical surroundings in their sensory dimensions. In our memories those places are stocked with sights, smells, sounds, people, and events that can be readily recovered and described.

A third way is to videotape an actual Sunday celebration and replay it for the group with the sound turned off. In this case the descriptive questions are limited to what we can see, to what catches and holds the eye, but this can be extremely effective.

An alternate technique to help us recover the experience of our liturgical surroundings is to actually visit the church, as individuals or as a group, to roam around in it and attend to our sensory impressions. It is helpful to go armed with descriptive questions to be answered immediately and shared with the group later. What about the surroundings strikes you most? Are there special sights, smells, sounds? Are there focal points to which your eyes go first, to which they always return?

Once we have recovered the experience of the liturgical environment in these or similar ways, we are ready to name the inner quality of the experiences we have described. Typical naming questions have to do with the feelings, memories, hopes, and dreams triggered by the sensory spaces. We are then ready to move on to the second phase.

Reflecting. The catechetical task in this phase is to ask ourselves what our experience of liturgical environment and the experience of others means, what it tells us.

The first thing to do is to reflect on the meaning of our own experience to which we have been attending in the previous phase. Though we might begin the reflection individually, at some point we need to reflect together as a group, to hear how our experiences coincide and vary, forming one personal-communal story.

The questions that lead the group into this kind of reflection on the particular sensory experiences described and named above are easily composed. What do those experiences tell us about our God? What do they tell us about ourselves, about how we form community, about our mutual relations inside and outside the assembly? Do they tell us what key values and actions we share? Do they tell us what those actions mean to us? What do they tell us about our world? What story do they tell us about where we've been and where we're going? This last kind of question is particularly helpful in leading us to weave the meaning we experience in liturgy into larger patterns and life stories. To each answer we give to these questions we need to pose a further question: Why? What was there about the sensory experience that suggests this meaning? How was that understanding voiced? This follow-up question is crucial. It helps us see that the meanings of the liturgy are truly embedded in the symbols we use and are not just imposed on them by our minds.

With this sense of what our experience means for us collectively we are primed to hear about the larger experience of our people. It is at this point that we can profit from the input of a resource person. Let me suggest several kinds of reflections on our larger story that can enlarge our perspective.

First, someone might help us search the Scriptures for passages to sensitize us to how the physical world around us reveals God to us. For example, Jesus draws frequently on his surroundings to reveal the presence and design of God's kingdom. Remember his words about those who see, but do not see? It is a question of learning to see beyond the physical, empirical reality. St. Paul offers a promising line of theological reflection in chapters three and four of 2 Corinthians. He speaks there of the glory of God shining on the face of Jesus, and of how our faces are transformed with that glory as we gaze on his face. The image that this passage, as well as the opening hymns in Colossians and Ephesians, brings to my mind is that of icon - Jesus as icon of God, ourselves as icons of Jesus. We might use this passage or the Gospel of John to explore the sacramentality of our world and our human existence exemplified most fully in the humanity of Jesus. Finally, the Old Testament prohibition of carven images has a healthy warning to sound.

Second, we might invite someone in the history of art, especially liturgical art, to explore the ways we have decorated our gathering places in the past - the use of light and dark, of mosaics, icons, and stained glass, of statuary and bas-relief carvings, of fabric furnishings and wall hangings, of incense and all that appeals to the senses.[3] The point here is not to do a detailed chronicle or study of technique, but to experience these artifacts as keepsakes that tell a portion of our history as God's people. A slide or visual presentation framed with reflective mood and commentary might do far more to unlock the environmental languages than straight lecture.

Third, the U.S. bishops' *Environment and Art in Catholic Worship*, especially the final paragraphs of section three, is worth another guided tour.

Fourth, liturgical artists from both fine and performing arts who can demonstrate or put into words how their art communicates are a resource we might also want to tap.

Here, as with the other kinds of input, our goal is to set our experience of the sensory spaces of our liturgical environment into the larger experience of our people across space and time so that our experience and theirs can interact creatively. Discussions about the meaning of our experience in the light of what we have heard flow readily at this point and bring this phase of the catechesis to a close.

Applying. The final phase of the catechetical process focuses on how we can apply what we have learned about our experience to our future celebration.

A first application can easily take place as part of the concluding reflective discussions. A newly honed sensitivity to the liturgical environment and its ways of speaking will likely suggest many follow-up attitudes and actions for us to implement in our future celebrations, both individually and collectively.

A second kind of application can be made by those who prepare and evaluate the liturgy.

PREPARATION AND EVALUATION

Liturgical environment, as we have been reflecting on it in this chapter, deals with the specific sensory ways in which a liturgical space speaks to the people who gather there for a particular celebration. Compared to liturgical space, which we considered in the previous chapter, liturgical environment is more changeable and in much more need of constant pastoral care by those who prepare the liturgy. This implies that attending to the environment will be a constant agenda item for the liturgy committee. Particularizing the environment for a given assembly and occasion can happen effectively only if the space has been kept flexible, as suggested in the previous chapter.

In preparing specific environments a liturgy committee will do well to adopt for itself a distinction made earlier between setting larger pastoral goals and doing the concrete preparation. Preparing an effective environment is one of the more delicate tasks the committee will perform. It is best given over to those who have both a feel and the necessary technical knowledge and skills to translate the mood and experience of an assembly and its celebration into sensory spaces. The committee serves these artisans best by establishing what mood and atmosphere it would like the environment to create and then stepping aside. Too many unskilled cooks easily spoil this broth.

In setting goals for the environment of a particular liturgy, the committee may find it helpful to spend time walking around in their assembly place to sense the ways in which it can resonate with the mood of the celebration and the people who are to gather for it. This is particularly true in getting the environment ready for special occasions and whole seasons. What the committee needs to communicate to the artisans is not the message of the liturgy, but rather its mood and the experience it hopes to evoke.

The committee also needs to be alert to a number of potential problems that can arise regarding the liturgical environment. The first stems from the fact that each sensory language communicates in its own unique way. One temptation we constantly face is that of reducing one sensory language to being a literal commentary on another. Slogan banners are one example, slides illustrating an intercessory prayer are another, musical mimicry of a ritual movement would be still another. Verbal language is especially prone to conscripting the other languages into being mere stress markers for words. Each language needs and deserves its own kind of space. The liturgy is meant to speak to us as one total language, richly and harmoniously varied. It seeks to evoke in us an experience of ourselves as God's people. We do better, then, to think of each sensory language as a unique and valuable way in which that experience is opened up to us in harmony with all the other languages being used.

A second potential trap springs from our successful use of the various sensory spaces. A liturgical design may have been so effective that we enshrine it and use it again and again. This is especially tempting when we have to create liturgical environments, a task which cannot be reduced to a neat, logical formula. It is so easy to pull out last year's successful lenten design for another run, ignoring the fact that the scripture readings and the circumstances of the assembly have changed. The cost factor may reinforce this temptation if quality materials are used.

A third potential conflict has already been noted at the beginning of this chapter. Visual and auditory space can be at odds with each other. Or the auditory space may not work well for both spoken and sung word. An attractive and visually prominent area where the eucharist is reserved for personal visit and individual prayer can distract from the communal gathering at table. Colors and objects meant to serve can end up overpowering a visual space. An un-renovated assembly space totally lacking in environment can easily contradict words urging full participation of the assembly spoken by ministers who inhabit a beautifully appointed sanctuary area.

A fourth problem is to find a proper balance between too much and too little change in the environment. Too much change makes it difficult, if not impossible, for the assembly to learn the particular variations of the sensory languages and to feel at home with them, and it endangers the assembly's sense of continuity with tradition. Too little change leaves us with a dull and stagnant environment, and it risks making the liturgy a museum.

There is no easy escape from these problems for a liturgy committee. We simply have to learn from our own, sometimes hard, experience and from listening with openness to what our people tell us about how they experience the liturgical surroundings. In the final analysis, the critical pastoral criterion for the environmental languages we shape is our people's ability to dwell in them.

As to resources, our own experience and that of our congregation should remain our most reliable guide in making the pastoral judgment regarding music or any art form. Many pastoral aids have been published to help us with everything from banners to lighting to seating arrangements.[4] These resources provide an excellent source of inspiration. Their strength is that they were written by pastoral experts. Their limitation is that they were written by pastoral experts who are not likely to know the specific needs and circumstances of our people. We cannot abdicate our pastoral role in preparing the kind of liturgical environment that will serve our people.

What, then, are the qualities we ought to look for as we prepare and evaluate the liturgical environments we fashion for the liturgy? Earlier chapters have already presented a number of more general qualities. Those are presumed here, and only a few more specific qualities need be added.

Norm: "The norm for designing liturgical space is the assembly and its liturgies" (EACW #42). The design should allow for the full verbal and non-verbal enactment of the liturgy and for the full bodily-spiritual involvement of the people.

Prepare and evaluate:

1. *Unity.* The liturgy is the action of a united people. Nothing, including the visually and spatially distinct areas which correspond to different roles and functions within the assembly, can be allowed to override a sense that this is the gathering place of the community; rather, "the wholeness of the total space should be strikingly evident" (EACW #53). Evaluation question: Was the environment unified?

2. *Human scale.* The liturgical environment should graciously welcome the people, without seeking to impress or dominate them. It should enable them to relate comfortably with one another as co-celebrants of the rite (EACW #52, 11). Was the environment hospitable?

3. *Prayerful scale.* The liturgical environment should facilitate the assembly's prayer and worship, inviting contemplation of God by its simple and attractive beauty (EACW #52, 12). Was the environment prayerful?

4. *Integrity and harmony.* The liturgy cannot be satisfied with anything less in its environment and all its artifacts and movements than an integral beauty which appeals to all the human senses (EACW #34). Were all the spatial languages used with integrity and harmony?

5. *Visibility.* The liturgical space must enable all in the assembly to see others and the ritual focal points, and it must create in the assembly a sense of the nearness, importance, and flow of the liturgical actions (EACW #49–50). Were the participants and liturgical actions visible?

6. *Audibility.* There should be an acoustical space conducive to both speaking and singing (EACW #51). Were all able to hear?

Summary question: Did the liturgy "appeal to the senses"? (EACW #34)

Notes

1. In preparing this descriptive essay I have relied in part on: Edmond Barbotin, "The Face and the Gaze," in his *The Humanity of Man*, translated by Matthew J. O'Connell (Maryknoll: Orbis Books, 1975), 225–285; Yi-Fu Tuan, *Space and Place. The Perspective of Experience* (Minneapolis: University of Minnesota Press, 1977), 161–178 and *passim*.

2. For a good discussion of the basically visual character of liturgical symbol, see: Nathan Mitchell, *Cult and Controversy. The Worship of the Eucharist Outside Mass* (New York: Pueblo Publishing Co., 1982), 367–423, esp. 375–383.

3. Those who have no access to resource persons and have to develop their own materials can find brief topical presentations in: *The New Catholic Encyclopedia* (New York: McGraw-Hill Book Co., 1967), 15 volumes; J. G. Davies (ed.), *A Dictionary of Liturgy and Worship* (London: SCM Press, 1972).

4. For some initial references see endnote #6 in the previous chapter. See also: Bishops' Committee on the Liturgy and The Catholic University of America Center for Pastoral Liturgy, *The Environment for Worship: A Reader* (Washington, D.C.: USCC Publishing Services, 1980).

3

Liturgical Time

IN THIS AND THE FOLLOWING CHAPTER WE WILL TAKE UP THE
second of the major liturgical languages, that of liturgical time. In
preparation for a closer look at liturgical times and seasons in the
next chapter, this chapter will consider the more elusive topic of
liturgical time as such.

THE EXPERIENCE OF LITURGICAL TIME

What is time?[1]

It seems so simple. We use time to identify the moment when
something happens. Or we use it to refer to a longer, measured
period during which a continuing event or a series of separate
events happens. We simply measure such time by calendars and
clocks. But is it that simple? Remember how hard it was to learn
to tell time as a child, to get the idea of what time is?

"What time is it?" It seems such an ordinary question. We check
our watch to see what time it is, according to Eastern Standard
Time, or Greenwich Mean Time, and we tell the time. Our
answer tells more than the time, however; it says that, true to our
kind, we are those who need to know and tell the time. That
question echoes down the ages. From "time immemorial,"
keeping track of time has been one of our human passions. From
Stonehenge and sundials and sentries crying out the hour, to
clocks with hands turned by weights or springs, to chronometers
with digital read-outs paced by the electric and magnetic oscilla-
tions of quartz crystals, ammonia molecules, and cesium atoms,

we humans search for ever more accurate ways to keep time for ourselves.

We "keep time" for ourselves. Time becomes a commodity, a vast, limitless resource for us. We save it, we spend it, we try to make it last. We live on "borrowed time." We "buy time." We don't have enough of it and are constantly "running out of time," or we have so much "time on our hands" we can't even idle it away. We learn to think of time as some thing that exists apart from us, out there.

We learn to keep time for ourselves more and more accurately. In the process we gradually come to measure time less by the inner movement of our own perceptions and human rhythms and more by the rhythms and recurring variations that pace movement and change in our universe, from supergalaxy to sub-atomic particles. The closer our watches match solar movements or atomic vibrations, the more we boast about how precisely and accurately they keep time. Subjective time gives way to a more objective, impersonal time.

We learn to measure time for our whole human family and our world as well. We love to begin pronouncements with "from time immemorial...." The "dawn of time" intrigues us. Geological time with its eons is almost beyond our imagination. We marvel at the truly astronomical "time" it has taken for our galaxy and universe to form and for its stars to send their light to us. Talk of "time warp" mystifies us. Time on so grand a scale leaves us feeling tiny and insignificant. Time on so vast a scale is an unseen, flowing tide within which our small solar system runs its course and we are swept along as we spend our fleeting days.

And so we end up seeing time as a thing, a sort of precise, objective measure that can be isolated and abstracted from ourselves and our world and used to measure the moments and the life span of everything and everyone. This kind of time does indeed exist, but it is a mental abstraction. Real time never exists alone. It is embedded in people and things. It is the moment of a happening or a human action, the duration of a life or a relationship or a physical process. The only way we can detect and measure real time is by comparing one event or process with another to tell when it happens and how long it lasts. Try as we might, we cannot completely eliminate ourselves from the time-keeping. We need, then, to take another look at time and ponder it in its human context, especially the kind of time that can be called human time.

Go back again to our starting point in childhood. We learn to tell time. After a lot of practice we are finally able to translate the movement of the sun across the sky or the movement of hands around the face of a clock into an hour of the day. Time does not speak itself. We tell it. Telling and keeping time are our human ways of dating occurrences in relation to ourselves or each other. "It happened when I was in college." "It happened [when I observed the hands of the clock] at four o'clock." In either case we are the point of reference, as participant or observer. In a real sense we center time on ourselves.

We each center our own time. Our life span reaches back and flows forward from our present moment. We move through that span, we fill it with our living. Time is not just something we have, it is that in which we are. Have you ever noticed how constantly we are asked to identify ourselves by our date of birth, by our age? These, along with our place of birth or residence, our sex, and our occupation, tell who we uniquely are. Or again, how we spend our time becomes an expression of who we are. Isn't that one of the purposes of a curriculum vitae?

Our human time, unlike the more precise, abstract time, is flexible and varied. We experience a constantly changing quality in time as it passes. Time flies or drags, according to our mood and involvement in what we are doing. We stretch out tender moments and good times. Some times are intense, peak moments; others are dull and uneventful. Time, even long periods of it, may seem to be without meaning. We endure the passing of such time. And there are other times, perhaps only fleeting moments, that seem filled to overflowing with a sense of meaning and purpose that spills over into the time that follows.

If we are attentive to our human experience of these changing textures of time, we can see that human time has its rhythms, its ebbs and tides. We experience it as a flow. We live in the present moment, but that moment flows out of a past time and into a future time. Or perhaps better, the past flows into the present and the future flows out of it. "Now" is a fleeting moment of transition between past and future which binds them together. "Now" is the moment of presence, to ourselves, to each other, to what is happening within and around us. It is the only moment we have to be whom we wish and to do what we want, but we cannot keep it. We can refuse to accept it and try to live in the past or the future. Each "now" quickly becomes part of the past. Those stored-up "nows" are our past; they have made us what we are, for good or ill. We possess them, in memory and in what we have become. But we cannot undo them, we can only reaffirm them or repent of them. And the future offers us endless hope and possibility. We dream about what we can be when the future becomes our "now." We anticipate it, we plan for it, but in many ways the future is also beyond our control - how much time we will have, whether the times will be good or bad. That is the paradox embedded in the flow of time. We shape our time, but we are also shaped by it.

In this we also see the seeds of how our lives take on meaning and consistency. We connect each thing that happens with the things that happened before and after it. We connect those events, in turn, with other things that happened before and after them, and soon we have strung them all together into a chain that spans a lifetime. The full meaning of each event can be found only in seeing it as part of what comes before and after. In a sense, each event is a summing up of past and future events. That is especially true of those things we experience as key moments, whether at the time or on later reflection. These moments of intense living have a way of gathering up the surrounding threads of our lives into a pattern of meaning. That is why we try to re-create those events, to prolong their impact. We constantly use them as marker events to sum up the story and direction of whole periods of our life, or of our life itself. In doing that we give our life a pattern, a story line. We put it together as a life history.

Such special times, both in their original setting and in their re-creation, feel different to us than other times. They are moments of intense living. We are caught up in their rhythm and flow, and time takes on a different quality for us. It's as though we have left our "ordinary" time and entered a time set apart, a "time outside of time" in which our whole existence is focused. That is why it is so hard to leave those special times and return to our ordinary lives. We linger as long as possible - over cordials after a meal with good friends, in the foyer of a concert hall after a powerful concert, in the stands after a stunning upset, in silent companionship with a friend when the talking has ended, in a family gathering after a long absence. We elevate such times into ritual events so that we can return to them again and again. And each time we do them anew they have a power to evoke our memories of the past, to anticipate our hopes and dreams for the future. They bring our lives together.

What we have been saying about our experience of human time applies not only to our individual experience, but also to our shared lives.

We center time together. "Before I met you...." Someone "offers me a future," or "holds the past against me." That song was popular before "our time." I have, or do not have, "time for you." "Let's spend some time together." Don't be a "two-timer." "Can I take a little of your time?" Our relationships begin and grow in time. It also takes time to repair the breaches and hurts between us. What we do in our time together is crucial for the relationship. But it's not just our actions that matter. Being able to take our time in doing them is just as important. To be willing to give up our own time center and let our lives be centered on another is the kind of wordless proof relationships feed on. Letting our lives be swept up into that of others involves risk. It is also, in part, what gives both love and discipleship their thrill.

Our time together is filled with events that bond us. Woven together in larger patterns, those events trace a common story we have shared, a common history we have lived. Again, as in our individual lives, it is this stringing together of events that gives them meaning. But now the story and its meaning embrace more than our isolated lives. The life story of the group reaches back to our ancestors, all the way to the dawn of our people's history, and forward to generations yet unborn.

We often extract that shared story entirely from its real times and places and sift out the perduring core of our group's experience. Thus freed to exist in a time beyond time, that story can come to life in any "now," whenever we remember it and tell it. "In the old country our ancestors were oppressed and had a hard life..." - thus we begin both family and biblical stories of our people. We introduce fairy tales and myths that catch the quick of human life with those familiar words that transport us beyond our present time: "Once upon a time...," "Long ago and far away...."

As in our individual lives, so in the life of the group there are special moments that seem to sum up our story. The founding events that set our course, moments of joy and danger when there was a heightened awareness of the group, events that led the group to new resolution or new directions - all these become marker events for us. We lift them out of their time and place and give them ideal existence in a ritual that can be celebrated again and again by the group. And when we celebrate them now, we leave our time and enter that ideal time of the group, a time beyond time. Or conversely, in ritual we re-embody that ideal time in our own time. "Thus we have always done...."

At this point in our reflection on human time we clearly stand on the doorstep to liturgical time, so let us turn to that experience.

What is liturgical time?

It is a time set apart from our ordinary time, a special time for gathering together to tell and enact our people's story. Like special human times, it is separated from surrounding time. We use entrance and dismissal rites to set it apart and to accomplish the transition from daily time into liturgical time and back again. And the liturgical time in between has a quality of its own.

Think, for a moment, of a liturgical celebration in which we are truly caught up. Something happens to draw us out of our normal preoccupations and leave us ready to hear God's word, to renew covenant with God. That is what the welcome by ministers of hospitality and the opening songs and prayers are meant to do. Celebration of word and sacrament can then unfold with an intensity that leaves us totally absorbed in what is happening. Time passes, but we hardly notice it. There is, rather, a sense of timelessness. We are caught up in the flow. And when such a celebration ends, we do not want to leave. It is only when we have acknowledged with thanks the goodness of what has happened, when we have been given a blessing to leave, when we have been charged to carry the meaning of that time back into our worlds, it is only then that we feel free to go. That is what the dismissal is meant to accomplish. Think, by way of contrast, of how none of this happens in those celebrations that fail to transport us beyond our ordinary world. Having never really left our everyday time, we leave the liturgical time easily, feeling no sense of uplift.

Good liturgy takes us to a time beyond time. That time is a special time in which our life stories and the life story of our people come together to form a whole, to gather up into a larger pattern the threads of meaning which often seem to be missing or scattered in the bits and pieces of our lives. But for that to happen we have to pay the same price we pay to be taken up into the life of another. We have to give up centering our own time and allow it to be centered on another, with others. The other who centers our time is the Crucified and Risen One. "Christ yesterday and today, the beginning and the end, the alpha and the omega. His are the seasons and the ages..." is our chant as we keep vigil and light the Easter candle. He centers our lives, and so it is his life story that must be told and enacted as the story of us all.

That, I think, is the implication of the three-year lenten cycle of readings given in the lectionary. The Gospels for the three years form a kind of triptych. In the middle panel we have the story of Jesus' journey to Jerusalem and Calvary on his way to the right side of his Abba. In the left panel we see the Gospel passages used in ancient days to prepare the catechumens for their baptismal journey with Jesus into the waters of death and new life. And in the right panel we find Gospel stories which model the penitential journey by which we renew our baptismal dying and rising with Christ. The church's express wish that we use the first panel of readings every year (ILM #97 [= #13 in DOL #1856]) clearly implies that we are to remember Jesus' story as our own story.

Permit me to offer a more theological reflection at this point. The heart of Jesus' story lies in his "hour," the time when he gives himself over and is accepted by his Abba. We call that the paschal mystery of his dying and rising. That "hour" began in our historical time, at three o'clock on a Friday afternoon, but it reaches completion in a time that is truly beyond time. And it is in that endless "now" that Jesus always lives to make intercession. We call that event the paschal mystery and we say that we celebrate it and make it present in our liturgies, in the outward symbols and actions we do. Are we not saying, then, that that timeless moment enters our liturgical "now" to become our moment, the summing up of our life?

One final thing needs to be added about liturgical time. We leave ordinary time to enter it. Setting apart a special liturgical time so that through it we may enter into a time beyond time is only one direction of the flow. In that same process the timeless moment when our story is summed up makes its entry into this special "now," and through that into the everyday "nows" out of which the liturgical time has been set apart. We also leave liturgical time and return to our ordinary human time where the dying and rising take place, not in liturgical symbol, but in flesh and blood.

What message does our experience of liturgical time convey? It tells us that we are a people who live in time, called to freely shape our times even as they shape us. It tells us that it is important to remember and recover again and again those special moments and key events that have made us a people. It tells us that we are a people with a past and a future, a people with a history. It tells us that the inner form of our story is given us in the story of the One whose new way we follow. It tells us finally that our time finds its center and resting place in the God beyond time who entered our time in Jesus of Nazareth. It tells us all this not by laying some abstract yardstick of time alongside our lives, but by enabling us to experience, in this special moment, that we live together with our God all the time of our lives.

CATECHESIS FOR LITURGY

As we begin this section, let us first note that doing a catechesis on our experience of liturgical time is far more difficult than catechesis on other, more concrete topics. The crux of the problem lies in the fact that time has an intangible character; we do not experience it directly. Some may find it easier to combine catechesis of this underlying experience of liturgical time with that of the more concrete experiences of times and seasons to be covered in the next chapter.

Attending. The first step is to recover, describe, and name our experience of liturgical time, to ask ourselves what we actually experience.

Liturgical time is very fragile. Forcing ourselves to become conscious of it while it is unfolding is the surest way to destroy its flow, to jar ourselves out of what anthropologists call "ritual awareness." Recovering it through a planned exercise is a delicate matter at best, since it so hard to insure that the experience will actually happen if we know ahead of time that it is supposed to.

One way that offers some hope of success is to begin the catechetical session with a type of prayer service which we know from past experience will be likely to succeed in drawing people into a time apart. The one I would suggest is some form of audio-visual prayer, since visual images, set in a basic symbolism of light and dark, are usually able to draw us into themselves. Use of music in a non-didactic way can enhance the experience. There should be no explanation beforehand other than giving the people whatever ritual cues they will need, and the aim of the service should be to evoke an experience, not to convey a message. In the study session that follows, the experience can then be explored in much the same way as we work with reminiscing. The advantage in risking this approach is that it provides us with a fresh, vivid experience on which to reflect.

Perhaps the most dependable way to recover our experience of liturgical time is through reminiscing. I would like to suggest two kinds of experience on which we can focus.

First, we have all experienced special times when we were so totally caught up in the flow of what was happening that our ordinary world faded away from our awareness. These times provide an excellent starting point to surface the unique quality such experiences have. When the people are in a reflective mood, have them go back in reverie to one or more such times. Special human times and special liturgical times can both be included. Have them dwell there and get the feeling of what was happening. Have them note who was there, what they heard and saw, how they felt, what spoke to them, whether the time seemed long or short, and in what ways those times were like or unlike ordinary time.

Once the experience has been recovered, we can process it individually and as a group. Our impressions can be gathered in response to descriptive questions. Again, we need to start first with our sensory experience. Naming questions can then serve to help us identify the inner quality of those experiences, the feelings, the memories, the hopes and dreams, the sense of ourselves and others. At that point we will be ready to move on to the reflection stage.

Second, we can focus our reminiscing on those special events that have become key events in our life stories. The purpose here will be to sort out how such events mark larger segments of our lives, how they unlock and sum up the meaning our lives have, how they help us sort out patterns and directions. Again, once we are in a reflective mood, we start by asking people to remember those events which have been most significant in our lives. Questions to lead people through such a memory journey are easily devised. When did the event take place? What were its circumstances? What went before and what followed after it? Who was involved? What made this event stand out from the time around it? What did it tell us about ourselves and our world? How did it influence our lives? Did the same kind of thing happen to us more than once? Were there other similar events?

Having re-lived those events, we can again turn to the descriptive and naming questions, individually and in a group, to recover the outer and inner dimensions of those experiences in preparation for the reflective stage.

Reflecting. In this step we ask ourselves what our experience and that of our larger community mean.

A great deal of sensitivity to the group is needed in this step. We do not find it too hard to share the kinds of special times we have isolated in the first reminiscing exercise above. We do find it much harder to lay bare those larger patterns in our lives which we explored in the final reminiscing exercise. It may be the first time we have tried to see our life as a whole, and we may feel very unsure of it. More importantly, we are too often convinced that we have no real life story to tell and we would rather remain silent than suffer embarrassment. Shared reflection on our life stories requires all the tact and skill a group leader can muster. But it is worth it in the end. There is no other way for us to discover that our lives follow common patterns despite the unique external details of our personal histories. And that is what we must do if we are to gain a sense of being a people. [2]

The task, then, is to reflect together on how we have experienced liturgical time and how it has shaped our lives. The questions we are to ask ourselves are all questions of meaning. What do the experiences of special times and of marker events tell us about ourselves, about our God, about being God's people, about the meaning and shape of our lives? And each answer that we give must be met with a gentle counter-question: Why? What concrete aspects of the experience tell us that? What is there about the experience that gives special times and events that kind of voice?

When a reflective awareness of how our experience of liturgical time speaks to us is in place, we are ready for a resource person to help us set that alongside the experience of the larger community. There are several potential areas from which input might be drawn.

First, scriptures offer us some leads. The experience of the sabbath is worth exploring for what it can tell us about the experience of a time set apart. [3] Someone well versed in scripture could also help us explore the christian sense of time and its relation to salvation history. This is also a good opportunity to get a larger sense of the pattern of Jesus' life story, which serves as our master story. The Gospel of Mark is especially attractive for its dramatic use of the journey motif. The continuing liturgical presidency of the Risen Lord in time beyond time, presented in chapter nine of the letter to the Hebrews where a parallel is drawn with Yom Kippur, also deserves reflection.

Second, when we draw on the past history of our people we might anticipate the materials of the next chapter. A particular feast or liturgical season can be explored for its way of shedding light on our human lives, whether in past or present experience. [4]

Third, a resource person might help us browse through the chapters on the liturgical year in Vatican II's *Constitution on the Liturgy* (#102–111 [DOL #102–111]) and in the *General Norms for the Liturgical Year and the Calendar* (#1–61 [DOL #3767–3827]) for the few hints we can find there.

Fourth, a professional story teller, if one is available in the area, can work marvels in helping us experience the power a story has to draw us out of our own time into a larger time.

Applying. The task of the final catechetical step, once we have seen our own experience of liturgical time in the perspective of our community's larger experience, is to ask ourselves what it means for the future celebration of the liturgy.

A closing discussion at end of the learning session will allow us to draw specific conclusions as to how we might participate more effectively in the liturgy in the future and use it as a basis for sharing a sense of common life story.

The liturgy committee may also want to take more account of the experience of liturgical time in its work of preparation and evaluation.

PREPARATION AND EVALUATION

In preparing and evaluating our assembly's experience of liturgical time, a liturgy committee would do well to attend to several areas.

First, the rites of gathering and parting, while secondary from the point of view of the main purposes of our liturgical gathering, are nonetheless critical in freeing an assembly to give itself fully to those purposes. We need to constantly hone our entrance and dismissal rites so that they will accomplish their pastoral task in an effective but unobtrusive way. It is important to realize that the designed rites cannot accomplish this alone. The warmth of ministers of hospitality in welcoming worshipers and bidding them farewell, provision for checking coats beforehand and lingering together in conversation over coffee and doughnuts afterwards, and other such seemingly minor details may be more important than we suspect in helping people make the transitions from daily life into the liturgy and back again.

Second, we need to pay more attention to pacing and rhythm within the central liturgical actions of word and sacrament. There are moments when it is psychologically important to spend more time and other moments that need to move more quickly. A bland, undifferentiated ritual in which everything is treated with equal importance easily leaves us feeling that nothing is important.

Third, we might well want to present the readings in a more overt story form. In this regard we have much to learn from oral interpretation and story theatre. Our pastoral aim in preparing the readings ought to be that we hear in them the master story of our people told once again in our "now" as our story. This holds as well for the homily which breaks open the readings.

In preparing and evaluating the quality of the liturgical time for our assembly gathering, the liturgy committee needs to attend to what the assembly actually experiences. It is not easy to ferret this out, but we need to constantly ask the question. We have no other choice. To date the experience of liturgical time as such has not received much attention, if any, in either church documents or liturgical literature. Our experience is practically our sole resource at this point.

What qualities can we look for in preparing and evaluating a good experience of liturgical time? Let me tentatively single out the following.

Norm: In the liturgy the people of God celebrate the sacred memory of Christ's saving work and the foretaste of his heavenly liturgy, joining their lives with his as they await his return at the end of time (CSL #7–8 [DOL #7–8]; GNLYC #1, 39 [DOL #3767, 3805]).

Prepare and evaluate:

1. *A gathering ritual.* Liturgical time is to be set apart by a gathering ritual which enables the assembly to move

more deeply into a time within and beyond their ordinary human time. Evaluation question: Did the entrance rite free the assembly to enter a time beyond time?

2. *A time outside of time.* Liturgy must so tell and enact the story of Christ as the story of the assembly that their human lives and times are totally caught up in its flow and they experience it as the story which gives the inner meaning of their lives. Did the liturgy lead the people to center their lives in Christ?

3. *A parting ritual.* Liturgical time is to be closed by a parting ritual which enables the assembly to return to their ordinary human time and infuse it with the meaning they have discovered it to have. Did the dismissal rite return the people to their ordinary lives renewed?

Summary question: Did the moment of liturgy transform the daily lives of the assembly with saving meaning?

Notes

1. An important source for this essay and for further reading is Edmond Barbotin, "Human Time," in his *The Humanity of Man* (Maryknoll: Orbis Books, 1975), 91–136. Additional material can be found in Roger Grainger, *The Language of the Rite* (London: Darton, Longman & Todd, 1974), 107–143; Yi-Fu Tuan, *Space and Place. The Perspective of Experience* (Minneapolis: Univ. of Minnesota Press, 1977), 118–135; and Arthur A. Vogel, *Body Theology. God's Presence in Man's World* (New York: Harper & Row, 1973), 66–86.

2. James B. Dunning, "The Stages of Initiation: Part I. Inquiry," in William J. Reedy (ed.), *Becoming a Catholic Christian* (New York: Sadlier, 1979), 104–105, quotes a conclusion Jean Haldane reached in her research, that the church is very good at telling people what their spiritual journeys ought to be, but that it seldom if ever listens to people or asks them to tell the stories of their own spiritual pilgrimage.

3. See especially the description of the sabbath experience given in Abraham Joshua Heschel, *The Sabbath: Its Meaning for Modern Man* (New York: Farrar, Straus, & Giroux, 1975).

4. For an example of how liturgical seasons can help us name our own experience, see Madeleine L'Engle, *The Irrational Season* (New York: Seabury Press, 1979).

4

Liturgical Feasts and Seasons

THE LAST CHAPTER DEALT WITH LITURGICAL TIME AS SUCH. In this chapter we will look at the concrete times and seasons that fill our yearly liturgical calendar. It is not our intent to study the historical origins and development or the liturgical structures of the christian feasts and seasons. There is abundant material, both scholarly and pastoral, at hand on those aspects. Rather, we will be concerned with the question of how we experience liturgical times and seasons.

THE EXPERIENCE OF FEASTS AND SEASONS

The experience we wish to explore here, from both human and liturgical points of view, is that of the time we identified in the last chapter as special time.[1] These are the times and periods that are in some way set apart from the ordinary time that surrounds them, a kind of time outside of time.

What are the kinds of time we're talking about?

Typical examples of special human moments and events are to be found all around us. Dawn with its invitation to a new day and dusk with its sense of closure are often special to us. They are the transition moments between day and night, light and dark, action and rest. We keep them special by transforming them into quiet times for personal reflection or a walk, a special time for family and friends, or the cocktail hour. There are other such times in the day which we also mark in special ways.

We also enshrine the important events of our lives, both in

memory and in anniversaries. The birth of a child, entering and graduating from school, coming of age, the first date, engagement, marriage, striking up a special friendship, getting a job and retiring from it, the death of a loved one - the list could go on and on. These events are special to us because of the ways in which they bond us to one another and shape our lives and our world. Because they are so special to us we remember and re-live the story over and over. We keep yearly anniversaries and are embarrassed if we forget. We hold reunions and gatherings that are filled with reminiscing about our times together and brought to a close with anticipation of the next get-together.

Events such as these also tend to center larger periods of time. Think of all the preparation and anticipation that lead up to a birth or a marriage, and of the basking in the experience that follows the event. The event makes the whole period special, and we fill that period with other ritual moments as well, with baby and bridal showers, with christenings and honeymoons and house-warming parties. There are many periods in life that hold special meaning and importance for us - childhood, adolescence, courtship, training for one's life profession, mid-life transitions, protracted illnesses. If we think back over such periods, we will see that there are many ways in which we ritualize and mark their unfolding, especially the central events.

Our history teaches us that we also use liturgical rites and celebrations to mark our special times. As we page through our past we find several cycles of celebration. There is a daily cycle, in which we have kept a "liturgy of the hours." The morning and evening have been pivotal times of prayer for us. More formal, psalm-centered prayer has served as the morning and evening prayer in religious communities and cathedral churches; more informal prayers said at one's bedside serve the same purpose in the family home. We also mark daily mealtimes with prayer. There is a weekly cycle, centered on our regular keeping of the Sunday feast. There is a yearly cycle with its high seasons of Advent/Christmas and Lent/Easter. And finally, there is a life-cycle of celebrations that accompany a christian from birth to death.

If we reflect on these special kinds of times and periods, we will see that they share certain characteristic features.

The first is the heightened awareness and intensity we noted in the last chapter. It may be that we have become so acutely aware of the joy and rightness of what is happening in our lives that we have to hold a feast, spontaneously devised if none is at hand. Or it may be that our lives are so muted and seemingly trivial that we need a feast to rouse us from our lethargy. Notice that in either case it is a question of meaning. We affirm the meaning and value that have become apparent, or we try to recover them for ourselves when they seem absent. The meaning and significance of our lives are normally something we only experience implicitly as we go about our daily activities. In lifting us to a moment outside of time our celebrations allow us to make that meaning explicit and say amen to it.

The second characteristic about special times is that they become recurring events. The meaning of our lives which is felt so powerfully in those moments cannot be allowed to die. And so we arrange reunions, anniversaries, memorials, and celebrations of various kinds to return to those moments. We may affix the feast to a recurring date or time of the year so that it becomes a cyclic feast, like a birthday, Thanksgiving, or Easter. Or we may time it to happen when our paths happen to cross, like the reunion of friends, or when the time is right, like the celebration of reconciliation. In those cyclic celebrations we re-enact in story and gesture the events that have bonded us and given meaning to our lives.

The third distinctive feature is that such feasts and seasons regularly take on highly ritualized patterns. When we go to grandmother's house for Thanksgiving, we know every detail in advance: who will be there, what sequence of things will happen who will do what, what the menu will be, what stories will be told. Christmas carols always begin at a certain time before the Midnight Mass, and the crib is always decorated the same way. We feel that the occasion has been spoiled if the pattern is disrupted. Patterns of action and significant objects used in the feast quickly become the keepsakes which must be brought out every year, for they enshrine in tangible ways the meanings we gather to remember.

A fourth feature worth noting is the deep feeling and mood that feasts and seasons have about them. These moods are shaded in subtly different ways and appear distinct only on closer examination. The simple joy of Christmas or of a christening to mark the birth of a child is not the same as the joy of an Easter eucharist or of a meal reuniting divided friends. When we borrow symbols and keepsakes from one feast or season to use them in another, they bring their memories with them. But they take on subtle new shades of meaning in their new setting.

Against that background let us turn to some examples of the four liturgical cycles we identified above, and take a brief look at how the experience of liturgical time is involved in them.

Prayer seems to flow so much more naturally at dawn and dusk each day. Why is that so? Those moments are the moments of break, of transition between night and day. The sun is the giant cosmic clock which marks them for us. From dawn to dusk the sun dispels the darkness and cold of night and replaces them with the light and warmth of day. Creatures of the day, we give the night over to rest, and the day to our action. This is the outward time we experience.

There is also an inner sense of time for each day, and it is not always the same from day to day. It has to do with the meaning and significance of what we do during the day. While the day is unfolding we are caught up in its affairs. But dawn and dusk are moments of pause. The more important to us the new day is, the more eagerly we face it at dawn. The more we have invested ourselves in the events of a day, the more we relish its completion and our rest when evening comes. There is another, more "primal" level. Dawn and dusk are fleeting moments of transition, neither night nor day. Anthropologists have long noted that such "in-between times" evoke in us deep feelings and a need to make that time a ritual time, for such times are moments of rich potential and great uncertainty. They strike a chord in us, for we, too, are in transition. Our lives are in constant flow, and such moments of pause leave us face to face with what we have been and what we might still become. That is why they are such particularly ripe moments for prayer - prayer of thanksgiving, longing, and repentance.

The weekly cycle of days, with Sunday at its head, is a less dramatic division of our time. Have you ever noticed how easy it is for the days to become alike when we suspend the routines that normally distinguish them for us? Days on vacation or in a novitiate easily become day, writ large. The seven-day week which we use in the West seems to have originated from the four phases of the moon as a way to divide the month, also a lunar measure of time. But we seldom attend to the phases of the moon now, except in jest. Our seven-day week now depends much more on human convention and has been shaped by Jewish and Roman tradition. The experience of outer time is in this case much less forceful, and that already alerts us to a pastoral issue concerning the Sunday feast.

What is our inner sense of Sunday within the weekly cycle? There are two aspects that seem to shape the way it feels to us. The first and more important is our long judeo-christian tradition. The Lord's resurrection on the first day of the week had marvelous overtones for the early christians. They already knew the sabbath as the commemoration of God's rest from the work of creation. The day after the sabbath now marked for them the beginning of the new creation. The eighth day symbolism of the Lord's rising has been with us ever since. Sunday became the premier day for christian gathering, a weekly feast to commemorate the Lord's rising.

The second aspect involved in our inner sense of Sunday time is our human need for a rhythmic pattern of days that allows our lives to breathe in and out. High energy and tension need to give way to relaxation. If we examine our Sundays carefully, we will note that they have a different quality than a normal workday during the week. It is not simply a matter of rest in the sense of inactivity. Studies have shown that we do many of the same things on Sunday that we do during the rest of the week. What is critical in our sense of Sunday rest is that we devote proportionately different amounts of time to those occupations, and especially that we apportion our time as we wish, without coercion.[2]

The yearly liturgical cycle, like the year itself, is based on our experience of solar time. The scientific explanation makes it sound so matter of fact. The earth tilts on its axis as it orbits around the sun over the course of a year, causing a shift in how long the daylight lasts each day, ranging from the shortest day of the year in winter to the longest day in summer. These are the winter and summer solstices. The days midway between these, when daytime and nighttime are equal, are the spring and fall equinoxes. The variation in sunlight, as light and warmth increase or decrease, helps create the seasonal rhythms in plant and animal life.

What a dramatically different quality this outer passing of time each year takes on when measured within our experience. It doesn't take our local TV weather expert ticking off the times of sunrise and sunset each day to let us know that the days are getting shorter and the sunlight dimmer as autumn fades into winter. And we know in our bones that some sort of dangerous low point has been passed when the light of the sun begins to lengthen and strengthen into the springtime. We know in nature around us and in ourselves the feel of new life in the spring, the robust vitality of summer, the mature harvest of fall, the death-like quiescence of winter. Is it any wonder that people everywhere mark such seasons of the year with stories and rites?

That is the experience on which the two seasons are built which highlight the yearly cycle of the liturgy: Advent/Christmas and Lent/Easter. Let us reflect briefly on each.

The outer time of Advent and Christmas is easily stated. The year's harvest has been gathered, and life around us ebbs and becomes dormant as the sun sinks lower on the horizon and the cold and darkness descend.

The inner experience of that time is another matter. In the long, cold night of winter, after the year's harvest has been gathered, we love to take our winter repose, to sit close together by the fire and tell stories of what has been and what we hope will be. Have you ever noticed the special mood that runs through the stories we tell and the songs we sing in our season of Advent and Christmas and asked yourself why? Gentle, winsome songs and stories they are, stories of human caring and mutual respect, filled with O. Henry's couple who give away their last prized possessions for each other, a Scrooge whom we can tolerate while we wait for him to see the light, a crippled boy whose ungainly jig is accepted as gift because it embodies a generous heart.

And why tell these stories and sing these songs at the darkest time of the year? Is it not to leave behind the incomplete and sometimes bitter human harvest of the dying year and to hope for what our human family still can be? The feast of Christmas, we know from historical research, was timed to the winter rebirth of the sunlight in order to enshrine not the actual date but rather the inner significance of the birth of the Savior.[3] In keeping this memory of the coming of a new Light into our world, are we not caught up in the future, dreaming of a day when the light of Christ will have dispelled all our human darkness and selfishness?

The season of Lent and Easter reaches back through Judaism's

Passover to two ancient springtime rites. On their way to summer pastures shepherds offered a lamb to ensure the fertility of their flocks. And the farmers offered unleavened bread baked from the first harvest of grain to secure the fertility of their fields. On first telling, those rites seem a bit simple and naive to us, though marvelously in keeping with our experience of the outer time of spring as a time of new life. We graciously imagine how the normal exuberance we all experience as life buds and sap rises could lead peoples of a simple culture to make such offerings.

The inner time they experienced is much more significant. In those cultures the life of the group hung in the balance every spring. It was literally a question of life and death. Would the new growing season bring enough food to keep them alive for another year? In offering bread and lamb they pleaded for and celebrated with joy the precarious gift of life in a semi-arid land. Is it any wonder that the Israelites transposed those rites into an annual memorial of that springtime when they were freed from slavery and given life as a people? And when a young Jew celebrated the passover feast of his ancestors with his band in an upper room in Jerusalem, it was that same gift of life, life in abundance, that he sought for all alike. The symbols were perfect for what he had to do. The Paschal Lamb must be slain, the grain of wheat must fall into the ground and die. Death is the price of life.

Death and life. In that context think back to the rich set of christian keepsakes that so lavishly adorn our lenten season. The dust and ashes of Wednesday speak of burnt hosanna palms and ruined cities and fertile ground, all in one symbolic breath. A new light piercing the darkness, altars stripped amid solemn liturgies, waters that can flood and drown as well as refresh and give growth - all symbols filled with the paradox of life and death. Lent is a time for giving up things and doing penance, for reading scripture and attending adult education talks, for extending alms to the needy and charity to one's own, for making one's Easter duty. In one way or another these practices all speak to us of leaving an old way of life and being renewed.

These symbols and practices are keepsakes we have inherited from the ancient church, from a time when Lent was first elaborated into a season under the influence of the community's way of initiating new members and re-initiating those who needed reconciliation. This is the same idea we met in the last chapter. The lenten lectionary tells the story of Jesus' dying and rising as its center piece. But this is flanked by the stories of our lenten journeys of initiation and reconciliation. Keepsakes and stories say the same thing. When we tell of and enact the paschal journey of Jesus, we tell and enact our own.

The final cycle includes those moments and periods of liturgical celebration which are timed to the cycles and rhythms of human life: birth, puberty and coming of age, entry into adult roles and states of life, illness and death. The "outer time" in these cases is be to found in physiological and sociological rather than cosmic processes.

If we think back over our experiences of such times of growth and change, we'll see that the processes involved reach beyond our physical body and our external relations to our group, and touch our very persons deep within. Those cycles and rhythms of change and growth have much to do with our developing sense of who we are, of whether we are valued and lovable persons capable of valuing and loving others, of what tasks are worth our life investment. We experience these seasons of our lives in many ways, as inner times of turmoil and struggle, as an age of new maturity and self-awareness, as a moment of inner restlessness or peace. We instinctively seek support and nurture at these times not only in passing moments of ritual, but also and especially in longer ritual processes.

Taken together those times are the milestones which mark the seasons of our lives. They give us our sense of direction and define our changing world for us. It is striking how many of our sacramental celebrations are associated with such times, whether by original design (e.g., marriage, ordination, anointing), or by practice (e.g., infant baptism, teen confirmation, eucharist as a universal context for other sacraments). It is also striking how often the rhythms and cycles of life are left critically unattended by any liturgical celebration specifically designed for that moment.[4]

The time of our lives is filled with an array of liturgical feasts and seasons. We keep them week after week, year after year, for a lifetime. What do they tell us? They tell us that our lives are process, that we remain the same person even as we change. They disclose for us the underlying pattern that is unfolding in the depths of all the moments and seasons of our daily lives to give them their final meaning. That pattern, liturgical feasts and seasons tell us, is the pattern of the paschal mystery first completed in the Lord Jesus. It is a pattern we all share.

CATECHESIS FOR LITURGY

Attending. The first task of catechesis on liturgical feasts and seasons is to attend to our experience. What do we and others actually experience then?

Recovering that experience is not at all difficult. There is a wealth of keepsake symbols and practices which have captured the mood of the feasts and seasons for us. We need only reminisce about them. That approach will suffice. Reminiscing about and describing the experience works well as a single process in the case of the feasts and seasons.

The first area we might reminisce about and describe is our human experience of time. When the group is gathered and relaxed, we can explore that experience, something done easily in full group. Lead questions might run as follows. What divisions of time are significant for you (week, month, quarter)? How do you think of and name your days? What events color the year for you? When does your year begin and end? What are its high points and low points? Are there discernible patterns? Questions like these will uncover our inner sense of time. Another interspersed question is needed to help us lift out the ways in which we ritualize those times and seasons. Are there special things you do to mark them? Such questions will evoke more than enough material for our further reflection in phase two of the catechetical process.

A second area for us to reminisce about and describe is our experience of liturgical feasts and seasons. Advent offers a particularly dramatic experience based on the time of the solar year. Questions to elicit the experience of the group can focus on our experience of light and darkness in the context of the diminishing daylight and lengthening nighttime, on the mood and special quality of the songs and stories of the season, and on its symbols and practices. Here, too, descriptions flow readily.

Lent offers an experience of a liturgical time rich in keepsake symbols and practices. People name them readily. Ashes, purple, fasting, the sound of clappers, bare altars, a kiss implanted on a cross, blazing fires and flickering candles, splashing water, fragrant scent of oil - all these symbols overflow with memories stored up and treasured for a lifetime and for centuries. Such memories are easily released for our reflection by a few simple questions.

Sunday might also be used as an example to help us get at our experience of a liturgical feast whose hold on us lies not so much in its power as a strong external time in the cosmic sense, but in its historical association with the Lord's rising and its inner memorial value for christians ever since. Descriptive questions can explore our religious and family observances and the reasons for them, as also our keeping of Sunday as a day completely at our disposal in contrast to workdays.

Having completed the process of reminiscing about and describing our experience of these kinds of special feasts and seasons, we can now ask the group to name the inner quality of those special times. Lead questions will focus on the moods and feelings triggered by the symbols and practices of the feasts and seasons. Ideas similar to those expressed in the essay section of this chapter should come easily. We all experience time from within. When we have named its inner quality, we are ready for the second catechetical task.

Reflecting. Our task in this second phase of catechesis is to ask ourselves what the experience we have named means to us and to our larger community.

We need first to collect the threads of meaning contained in our own experience of liturgical feasts and seasons. Once again, the questions will center on what these special times tell us about God, about ourselves, about our journey and history as God's pilgrim people. They will naturally focus on the specific, concrete ways in which the feasts and seasons give us a sense of pattern in our lives and in our journeys of dying and rising. Given what we have noted above about the subtle shades of meaning and mood found in such special times, we should be prepared to spend time drawing these out. The follow-up question remains critical: Why? What is there about the experience of a feast or season that enables it to speak to us in that way?

Our collected sense of our life seasons can then be set alongside the experience of the larger community with the help of a resource person.

First, scriptures provide a superabundance of materials on the origins and early development of our feasts and seasons in the experience of the Jews and the early christians.

Second, the later historical developments of those feasts and seasons have also been widely researched and reported.[5] Setting the symbols and practices back into their original settings can help us name and unlock a depth of meaning we have felt in them but perhaps never put into words.

Third, someone familiar with the *General Norms for the Liturgical Year and the Calendar* (DOL #3767–3827) might be asked to give us a highlight tour, to lift out the underlying sense of liturgical times and seasons contained there.

Fourth, we ought not neglect the rituals and practices of popular religiosity that are found in many of our communities. Someone versed in these practices and their history can help us see how others embody their experience of themselves in festal times and seasons.[6]

In seeking input the goal to keep clear for ourselves is our need to see our experience of liturgical times from the perspective of the larger community, so that our experience can be challenged and creatively enlarged. That will prepare us to apply what we have learned more effectively.

Applying. The third catechetical task is to ask ourselves how what we have learned applies.

The above steps will normally uncover many new ideas and areas of awareness. A concluding discussion is of great help to the group in sorting out and choosing follow-up actions we may wish to take, both for our own heightened participation in the liturgical feasts and seasons and for the community's celebration of those times.

Implementation of the ideas for a heightened community celebration of feasts and seasons will normally be the work of the liturgy committee when it does its preparation and evaluation.

PREPARATION AND EVALUATION

Feasts and seasons are one of the constant agenda items for a liturgy committee. The liturgical times bring together in a unique way both the memories of past traditions and the assembly's inner experience of our own time. Preparing and evaluating feasts and seasons offers the committee an unparalleled opportunity to help the assembly bring the tradition to life in our day.

As they prepare liturgical seasons a liturgy committee may want to take up a process recommended earlier, that of preparing an entire season at one time and well in advance.[7] The scripture readings given in the lectionary for each season were chosen as a series to fit the season. Preparing for an entire season allows us to build on the themes of those readings. Similarly, that way of preparing enables us to develop and subtly alter symbolic motifs and moods over a period of weeks and thus build up a sense of anticipation as we approach the feast.

In preparing feasts and seasons the committee will also want to pay close attention to the assembly's sense of tradition and familiarity with the practices and symbols used. Feasts and seasons tend to be more highly ritualized than ordinary liturgical times, and symbols and practices sustain our memory of the feast's meaning from year to year. The symbols and practices should have a feeling of being known.

This does not mean that we are locked into repeating literally what we have done in the past. Both the scripture readings of the liturgy and the living experience of the assembly change from year to year, and our preparation must be responsive to those changes. Symbols and practices are not to be repeated woodenly. With a little sensitivity and care they can be retained but subtly altered to pick up the new mood of the readings and the assembly. It is not a question of creating a new set of symbols, but of doing variations on a theme.

Pastoral resources abound to help us with the task.[8] Aids such as these are a rich source of inspiration. In the end, however, it is ours to make the final pastoral judgment about celebrating the tradition's feasts and seasons in a way that speaks to our assembly.

What qualities ought we look for in preparing and evaluating our celebrations of the feasts and seasons?

Norm: The liturgical year with its feasts and seasons recalls and "unfolds the whole mystery of Christ" and thus makes the mysteries of redemption "present in every age in order that the faithful may lay hold on them and be filled with saving grace" (CSL #102 [DOL #102]).

Prepare and evaluate:

1. *Centrality of paschal mystery.* The paschal mystery, which sums up the whole of Christ's saving work, is the

moment which centers all liturgical celebration of feasts and seasons and provides the paradigm which gives meaning to all inner experience of human time. Evaluation question: Was the paschal mystery truly the focus of the celebration?

2. *Balance of memory and hope.* In keeping liturgical feasts and seasons we are called to remember the historical saving work of the Lord Jesus, experience its presence now, and await its fulfillment in hope (CSL #102 [DOL #102]; GNLYC #1 [DOL #3767]). Keeping them as "historical anniversaries" is not sufficient; memory must be balanced with a sense of incompletion and longing for the day of the Lord's return. Was the assembly led to remember and hope?

3. *Open to human time.* To make the paschal mystery present in every age so that the faithful may lay hold on it requires that feasts and seasons be celebrated in such fashion that they gather up our human experience of time. Was the celebration truly responsive to our human experience of time?

4. *Open to present age.* To make the paschal mystery present to this age, to the particular people gathered to keep feast, the liturgy must provide both common and special celebrations which speak to them in their own moments and periods of struggle and growth in a lifetime of following the way of Jesus. Was the liturgy truly responsive to the moments and seasons of those gathered?

Summary question: Did the liturgy celebrate the moments and seasons of a christian's life?

Notes

1. Not much has been written on the question of how we experience liturgical times and seasons. Some leads can be found in Adolf Adam, *The Liturgical Year: Its History and Its Meaning after the Reform of the Liturgy* (New York: Pueblo Publishing Co., 1981). Another unexpected work that can trigger reflection on our experience of the liturgical year is: Madeleine L'Engle, *The Irrational Season* (New York: Seabury Press, 1977).

2. See William C. McCready, "The Role of Sunday in American Society: Has It Changed?," in Mark Searle (ed.), *Sunday Morning: A Time for Worship* (Collegeville: Liturgical Press, 1982), 97–119.

3. Liturgists who live and work in the southern hemisphere, where the feast occurs when the summer sun is at its height, face a difficult task in translating this feast into their own experiential context.

4. For an overall treatment of the stages of adult life and the invitation each offers to christian faith, see: James W. Fowler, *Becoming Adult, Becoming Christian: Adult Development and Christian Faith* (San Francisco: Harper & Row, 1984); James W. Fowler, *Stages of Faith. The Psychology of Human Development and the Quest for Meaning* (San Francisco: Harper & Row, 1981); Evelyn Eaton Whitehead and James D. Whitehead, *Christian Life Patterns. The Psychological Challenges and Religious Invitations of Adult Life* (Garden City: Doubleday, 1979).

5. See: Adolf Adam, *The liturgical Year: Its History and Its Meaning after the Reform of the Liturgy* (New York: Pueblo Publishing Co., 1981); Laurence F. X. Brett, *Redeemed Creation. Sacramentals Today (Message of the Sacraments* 8) (Wilmington: Michael Glazier, 1984), 51–97; Peter G. Cobb, "The History of the Christian Year," in Cheslyn Jones, Geoffrey Wainwright, Edward Yarnold (ed.), *The Study of the Liturgy* (New York: Oxford University Press, 1978), 403–419; Thomas J. Talley, *The Origins of the Liturgical Year* (New York: Pueblo Publishing Co., 1986); Robert E. Webber, *Worship Old and New* (Grand Rapids: Zondervan, 1982), 161–173; James F. White, *Introduction to Christian Worship* (Nashville: Abingdon, 1980), 44–75.

6. See Dionisio Borobio, "The Four Sacraments of Popular Religiosity," in Luis Maldonado and David Power (ed.), *Liturgy and Human Passage* (*Concilium*, 112) (New York: Seabury Press, 1979), 85–97.

7. See Yvonne Cassa and Joanne Sanders, *Groundwork: Planning Liturgical Seasons* (Chicago: Liturgy Training Publications, 1982).

8. See, for example: the series edited by Gabe Huck, entitled *Major Feasts and Seasons* (Washington, D.C.: Liturgical Conference, 1975–1977); Gabe Huck, *The Three Days. Parish Prayer in the Paschal Triduum* (Chicago: Liturgy Training Publications, 1981); Daniel Coughlin, *Parish Path through Lent and Eastertime* (Chicago: Liturgy Training Publications, 1981); Maryann Simcoe (ed.), *Parish Path through Advent and Christmastime* (Chicago: Liturgy Training Publications, 1983).

5

Liturgical Action

WE TURN NOW FROM THE MORE HIDDEN LITURGICAL LANGUAGES OF
space and time to the more overt languages of action and speech,
which lie at the core of the liturgical event. The liturgical
language of action will be the subject of the next two chapters.
This chapter will focus on movement, posture, and gesture; the
following chapter will consider the use of liturgical objects.

THE EXPERIENCE OF LITURGICAL ACTION

An observation offered at the beginning of the chapter on
liturgical environment, based on people's experience of the new
liturgy, seems equally pertinent as we begin our reflection on the
experience of liturgical action.[1] If we listen carefully to how we
describe our experience of the renewed liturgy in contrast to the
old liturgy, we cannot help but notice two things. The new
liturgy communicates a healthy sense of community, full participation,
and mutual service within the assembly, but it falls far
short of the sensory impact of the old liturgy. In comparison our
liturgy is now a very wordy, disembodied liturgy. The remedy is
obvious enough. We need to attend more to the sensory
environment of the liturgy and to the bodily actions which are an
essential ingredient of the liturgical celebration. For actions do
what the words say; in bringing about meaning they communicate it in a way that words cannot.

What kinds of bodily action are we speaking of?

An inventory would include the various postures we assume,

the gestures we make, and movements from place to place. Gestures cover a whole range of movements of facial muscles, head, limbs, and body which we use to express, emphasize, or evoke thoughts, feelings, and moods, either in company with speech or alone.

Are such human actions truly a language that communicates?

Our first, offhand impression is that we communicate by words. When we act, we seek to accomplish practical purposes, such as manufacturing a product, preparing a meal, or making a living. At other times we act for the sake of relaxation and leisure, as when we take a vacation or a nap, play a game, or go dancing. Words say things, actions do things.

But is the distinction that neat? If we take another look we'll see that our words accomplish things, too, and that our bodily actions cannot be reduced to just doing our work or taking our leisure. Take an obvious case of verbal communication, like talking over a telephone. Have you ever caught yourself smiling to the party on the other end of the line or making a gesture to describe something or emphasize a point while you were on the phone? We may feel momentarily embarrassed over such actions, but they serve to reveal how integral bodily actions are to our communication process. Or have you ever wished, while reading letters from friends, that you could see their expression or hear their tone of voice to get the full meaning of what they were saying? Or again, does the mechanical tone of a simulated human voice coming out of a computer or a cash register at the supermarket check-out counter ever strike you as funny? These simple experiences tell us that human communication is much more than a purely verbal process. It involves our entire bodies.

In recent decades the discipline of social psychology, especially the branch sometimes called "kinesics" (the study of human movement), has pioneered the study of how we communicate through our bodies. It is from those studies of human behavior that we have learned to speak of "body language." It is worth our while to review a few of their findings.

Human communication, they have found, is a multi-channel phenomenon. We vocalize only a small percentage of the time we are together, but communication goes on constantly. The verbal channel is not the only means we use. Each of the senses provides us with another channel. Touch is one of the most satisfying and psychologically important channels of communication, one that we especially use with close friends and family. Smell and taste seem to have less importance in our culture. Sight is the channel we use most constantly. We use it in a variety of ways. We maintain eye contact and gaze at the face of others to catch their expressions and change of moods. We subconsciously watch their bodily gestures and postures to read their feelings. The actions we see them perform strike sympathetic chords in us and we mirror those actions in our own bodies. Couples and friends who are attuned to each other adopt the same postures and move their bodies in sympathetic response to each other. And aware that we are seen by others, we quickly learn to act in certain ways in their presence. Human communication, then, is a multi-channel affair.

These channels, the studies have found, are interdependent. Each works together with the others to form a total system of communication. We often depend on one channel to modify or substantiate what we say with another. A wink takes the sting out of a teasing word. Touch makes up for the inadequacy of our words of compassion to one who suffers. There is, then, a redundancy in our total communication system, with the same message and meaning repeated through the different channels. But it is not a simple, mechanical repetition. Each form of sensory communication adds a unique dimension to our communication and reveals a facet of meaning which the others cannot. Words clarify and speak plainly, touch wordlessly affirms our desire to be as near to another as we can be in whatever they are feeling, sight distances and objectifies even as it becomes gaze and acknowledges the other as a person like ourselves. We impoverish our human communication if we try to restrict it to a single channel.

Studies have also noted how our bodily actions link together to form larger wholes. Like the sounds and words and sentences that build up our verbal language, small units of action are linked to others to form "words" and "sentences" and "paragraphs." Nor do our actions occur in isolation. One person's action triggers the action of another in response. That response does the same, and soon a chain of interaction is built to bond us. To understand what we are saying with our bodies we must see our actions in context and in sequence, as part of a larger, unfolding interaction with others.

Social psychology has rightly taught us to think of bodily action as a language. So we need to reflect further on its character as a body language, that is, as a form of human communication that happens in and through bodily action.

Let us start with the fact that it is a *body* language. The body is its vehicle of communication, and every bodily action we perform has the potential to say something about ourselves to others.

Why is this so? How does it happen? We find the answer in how we experience ourselves. Even though we may see the image of our bodies in a mirror or touch another part of our bodies with our hand, it is still from within ourselves that we see our bodies and know what they are like to our touch. Furthermore, biologists tell us, we have a marvelous inner sense called kinesthesia by which we experience our bodily movement from within. This sensation is produced by special fibers and nerves in our muscles and joints which tell us that we are running, or smiling, or sitting erect, or reaching out with our hand. Or better, by kinesthesia we feel the smile or the frown on our face, we feel tall or bent when we stand tall or stooped, we feel swift or labored when we run. We feel these things from inside ourselves.

Let me take this one step further. It is not just a physical experience of our bodies that we get from within. We feel open or closed inside when we lift our head and smile or lower it and frown. We feel inwardly alert and ready to act when we stand tall, we feel closed and resistant when we hunch our bodies or double over. We feel free when we run or dance. Our bodily actions express or evoke human feelings deep within us.

That is the heart of the matter. We experience that we are an outsides and an insides. Our bodies are our outsides. Our feelings, our hopes, our fears, our awareness, our freedom - all these make up the mystery of what we are within. Or to use more familiar terms, we are body and spirit, we are an enfleshed spirit, an inspirited body. That is the way we are made up, and that is what determines how all our communication with others of our kind takes place. We do not commune directly, spirit to spirit. Rather, for communication to take place what is within us has to press its way outward through our bodies, to express itself in some fashion. And that outward, bodily manifestation of what is within us has to impress another, to press its way inward through their bodies. Therein lies the necessity and the paradox of our bodily communication. Our inner mystery, the persons we are within, can only be disclosed to others through our bodies, bodies that can hide as well as reveal what is within us.

What this means is that we are each walking sacraments. The body is the outward symbol which tells of and makes present a hidden, inner reality. This means that each of our bodily actions has the potential to reveal and present something of ourselves to others, or to hide and withhold it from them. This also helps us understand how bodily action communicates. What we do in the body mirrors what is within. The body acts as an icon of our inner attitudes and sentiments. The act may also call that inner attitude into being. Think of a handshake or an embrace. What happens physically is that we open our hand or our arms and enfold the hand or the body of another within ours. But something deeper happens. In clasping hands or embracing we open ourselves within to take in, not just the body of the other, but his or her very person. Again, this is something the body does. We do not have to put it into words, though words may be added to say the same thing. And we sense when a handshake or an embrace is insincere and without meaning, no matter what the words may say.

From our individual point of view this kind of bodily action accomplishes something marvelous in us. Because it engages us fully and simultaneously as body and spirit, it integrates us and gives us a sense of wholeness in a way that neither purely external or purely internal action can. When we act so as to reveal and offer to another through our bodies what we are within, we are whole and complete. There is another aspect of that integration to note. Bodily action, mental awareness, feelings and emotions, free self-disposal - all the dimensions of our human existence work together in harmony. That is why enacted meaning is most apt to be a meaning that is felt. In the moment of acting, reasons and attitudes of the mind become inner attitudes and reasons of the heart as well; we commit ourselves and take a stand on what we know and feel.

Something further needs to be said about our using bodily action as a body *language*. Movements and gestures are not restricted to being stress markers, exclamation points, or non-verbal illustrations for the words we use. They can serve those purposes. But they also speak in their own right when we string them together in larger wholes as a form of social interaction; they say what cannot be adequately put into words.

One of the most basic things movements, postures, and gestures say to us is that we are body-persons capable of communicating with others. That ought not be misinterpreted to mean that we enter life as fully formed persons who have an option to communicate or not. If we attend to our experience of bodily interaction with others, we discover that we become the persons we are through that interaction. We learn from the caring touch of a parent that we are valued and loved, and that incites in us the ability to value and love others in return. The attentive, engrossed look on the face of a conversation partner encourages us to share and develop the feelings and ideas within us. The forgiving hug of a friend loosens in us an unsuspected power to forgive. A hand stretched out to us in a moment of need teaches us how to rise above self-concern in dealing with others. In a word, we are called forth to become the persons we are by the deeds of others. Bodily interaction opens up to us the possibility of going beyond our limitations and transcending ourselves.

Our bodily interactions also bring a fuller integration beyond the one we spoke of above. When we see in others the bodily postures and gestures that express so well the feelings we remember experiencing in ourselves, or when we are incited to act in the same way and in so doing come to feel what they feel, we sense our shared humanity. In that moment we know that we are not just isolated individuals, but a whole, corporate humanity. We know that others are "flesh of our flesh, bone of our bone," that the same inner experiences course through our lives.

That brings us to what is perhaps the most important thing body language communicates among us. It is the vehicle by which we share common values and attitudes, the same felt meanings, and our sense of mutual roles and relationships. We need only observe the formative practices of families, religious communities, and other groups in which an individual is totally immersed, to see how constantly and instinctively we rely on the imparting of the ways of the group to perpetuate the bonds and common values of the group. We are and remain family or friends because of the many things we do together; we easily drift apart when we stop doing things together. Because body language is largely something we learn from our elders and leaders by imitation, without ever consciously attending to it, it tends to resist change and to perpetuate the attitudes and values it embodies over long periods of time.[2] The more important those attitudes, values, and relationships are to our group's survival, the more we ritualize and formalize the behaviors in which they are embedded.

Against that background we can now turn to our experience of liturgical action as a language.

What kinds of liturgical actions are we speaking of?

We perform many expressive bodily actions during the liturgy that are not of concern to us here, such as personal behaviors, spontaneous interactions with those next to us, or acts of social decorum. We are concerned rather with those actions that are called for in the liturgy as part of our ritual interaction. Included in our inventory of such actions are various kinds of movement, posture, and gesture. Members of the assembly move between the various seating places and focal places of liturgical action (lectern, font, table), often in the form of a procession. Liturgical postures include standing, sitting, kneeling, and prostrating. Among the gestures called for in the liturgy are bowing, genuflecting, signing oneself, folding or raising one's hands, a handshake or embrace of peace, making eye contact, and touching. Other actions and gestures, especially the sacramental gestures of the presider, make use of objects and will be considered in the next chapter.

How are these actions, already communicative as human actions, transformed when used as a liturgical language?

If we think back over our experience of these liturgical actions, one of the first things we notice is that they are fewer in number, more constant, and more stylized than the variety of bodily actions we use in our human communication. The size of the gathering has much to do with this. The facial displays and casual gestures we fashion so freely and spontaneously in intimate settings with family and friends are not large enough for larger groups of people, whether human groupings or a liturgical assembly. And so we select certain actions and enlarge and stylize them, in much the same way we do in theater performances or public rallies. But there is another reason as well. These actions are our community's hallowed ways of embodying, generation after generation, those shared values and the sense of meaning that root and identify us as a people. They may even trace their origins to the founder, who left an example or a command, "Do this...." It is only natural that we stylize and care for those gestures that tell us who we are.

Another thing we discover about our liturgical actions, like their counterpart human actions, is that they occur in clusters and usually in connection with words. Baptismal bathing is joined to acts of anointing and clothing. Imposition of hands and signing with the cross often go together. Standing with head and hands upraised accompanies one kind of prayer, kneeling with head bowed and hands folded marks another. And, as in this last example, words are often joined to actions to repeat their meaning. When each language is kept intact, such clustering provides a rich, multi-faceted liturgical experience. If one liturgical language is allowed to dominate, as often happens with words, the others atrophy and become mere formalities, paradoxically leaving the dominant language impoverished as well.

Reflection on our liturgical actions also tells us that they consist of basic kinds of human action set in a context of prayer. In this new setting the meaning they already have as a human language remains as a basis for and is transformed into a new meaning. A simple exercise enables us to check this out for ourselves. Assume several traditional prayer postures in succession. But spend time with each, first to identify the physical sensation of the body in a certain posture, then to ask what mood that posture creates, and finally to ask what our prayer would be if we were to pray in that posture and mood. It is amazing to discover how the physical and psychological experience of different postures will suggest different kinds of prayer. The process at work here is the kind of iconic function of the body which we named earlier. Prayer said standing with head and hands upraised becomes prayer of praise and self-commitment. Bended knees and bowed head plead and repent. Raised hands speak of hearts lifted up to God. A handshake or an embrace offers a peace which the world cannot give. Hands folded as mirror images of each other bring an inner quiet and peace of soul. Sitting hollows out in us a lap-like receptivity to receive a word in faith.

Most important of all, reflecting on our experience discloses a mystery in our liturgical actions. They begin as address and response among the members of the assembly - a language we speak to one another. But they embody something more, for God becomes the assembly's dialogue partner in that exchange. We greet each other with words and outstretched arms. What we wish and offer is not merely our human presence to each other. "The Lord be with you ... And also with you." We hear words spoken to us by a human voice and we say "The Word of the Lord ... Thanks be to God." We exchange human gestures of peace after we have remembered in prayer the promise of a peace which only the Lord can give. We offer someone bread, which normally symbolizes the giver's human body for which it is meant, and say "Receive the Body of Christ." We bow our heads to receive God's blessing from human hands. We sign ourselves to say we are on a cross with Christ. The mystery is this, our human actions speak and act for God, bodying forth God's presence to us. Conversely, we also know from experience how little sense of God's presence we feel when liturgical actions are performed without care or prayer, as mere rubrical prescriptions. Such actions say little or nothing of God.

What, then, is the unique message of the language of liturgical action? It tells us that we are whole humans, singly and together. It tells us that the bodies we are and the Body we are are holy. It tells us that our God is a humble God who has drawn near to us in the body of Jesus and in our bodies. It tells us that our bodiliness is not an unseemly, impenetrable barrier between ourselves and God, but rather the bearer of God's holy presence. Words can say these same things; only a body language that acts them out can convince us of their truth.

CATECHESIS FOR LITURGY

Attending. The first task of liturgical catechesis is to attend to the movement, postures, and gestures we use in the liturgy, to put ourselves in touch with what we actually experience through our bodily involvement. Toward that end we need to recover, describe, and name our experience.

Recovering the experience can be done through a form of reminiscing in which a leader guides us through a past experience of the liturgy. The leader will need a carefully prepared, sequential list naming in detail the things that happen in the chosen type of liturgy. When the group has assembled and been helped to enter a mood of reverie, we are then taken through the liturgy, action by action, and asked to identify with a descriptive word or phrase what we felt at each of those moments. It is important that the leader simply name the actions without suggesting what what we ought to have felt. We are left free to describe what we experienced, if anything. This exercise begins with each of us answering the question for ourselves. Sample answers can be shared in the group later. An alternate technique might be to watch a videotape of a liturgy we attended with the sound turned off or to do a reminiscence based on the poetic reflections on liturgical gestures published in the magazine, *Assembly.*[3]

A highly effective way to recover our experience of liturgical action is to isolate and perform those actions in a prayerful, reflective setting. Let me describe a technique a colleague and I have developed.[4] It is like what we used to call a "dry mass." We select a liturgy, usually the eucharist or a portion thereof, which the group celebrates together in all its details with only one exception: no words are used. At times we will have the group do two eucharists, one a typical Sunday celebration with the group scattered throughout the church, doing what they normally do. The other, for the sake of contrast, is done at a later time in a more intimate, circular setting, and the participants are first taught a simple gestural language of greeting, praise, thanks, petition, amen, etc., based on the rubrics for ministers, to substitute for spoken responses. In addition, a "deacon" leads them by miming their responses. In either case it is important that all in the group make an earnest effort to pray. In the follow-up group discussion descriptions of what we experience come tumbling out.

An easier and equally effective technique for recovering our experience of liturgical actions is to have the group go through a series of prayer postures and gestures.[5] The exercise is best done with music in the background, without words except for the guidance of the leader, and with eyes closed. It helps to start off with an exercise to help us center and become aware of our bodies. Then we can leisurely move through the postures and gestures, taking time to ask ourselves three questions with each one. What does my body feel? What mood does that create in me? If I were to pray now, what would my prayer be? In the ensuing discussion, members of the group can be asked to describe what they experienced.

Describing our actual experience of the bodily action of liturgy will have already been part of each of the above exercises. At this point in attending to our experience one final thing remains to be done, to name the inner quality of that experience, the moods and feelings it caused in us.

Reflecting. The second catechetical task is to reflect on the experience we have gathered and named, to ask ourselves what it means. The aim of this task is to help us integrate the bits and pieces of our experiences into larger, shared wholes.

The first phase of the reflection has us look at the meaning of the experience to which we have been attending. We ask ourselves what that experience tells us about our God, about being God's people, about how God interacts with us, about the values we hold dear, about the bonds that tie us to each other and our world. And as we give our answers to these questions, we must always ask ourselves the counter-question: Why? What is there about the bodily actions of the liturgy that enables them to say these things? These counter-questions help us lay bare the sacramental structures of the liturgical actions.

When we have shared the meaning of our experience in that way, we are ready to hear from a resource person the story of how our larger community has experienced those same actions.

Scriptures offer a variety of possible topics. Exploring the ritual practices which our liturgy has inherited from Judaism and the early community can give us many new insights as to their meaning. Or again, someone might help us search the Gospels to attend to the deeds and actions of Jesus, asking ourselves what they have to say about the kingdom. Finally, along a more theological vein, a biblical reflection on Jesus as the enfleshment (incarnation) of the divine Word, who reveals God in the flesh and models all encounter with God, can help us root the bodiliness of our liturgy.

Someone acquainted with the history of the liturgy can help us attend to how the shape and meaning of the rites have grown and evolved over the course of the centuries. The recital of our history need not be detailed. What is more important is to capture a sense of how the liturgical postures, gestures, and movements have spoken to us in different times and circumstances. This kind of story-telling reveals the values and meanings invested in our community's ways of doing things. It is our most persuasive means of perpetuating a sense of continuity with the past and at the same time opening ourselves to the need to allow our ways to continue to change.

The fourth section of the U.S. Bishops' *Environment and Art in Catholic Worship* (#55–62) also offers some useful materials.

Finally, performing artists with teaching experience in the fields of dance, body movement, and theater can also help us explore our experience of liturgical postures and gestures. As part of their service to us, they might also be called upon to help us design and conduct the kinds of attending exercises described above.

In each case, we bring the reflective task of catechesis to completion by having the group place what we have learned through the input alongside our own experience, so that our experience can be broadened and challenged by what we have heard.

Applying. The final task of catechesis is to ask ourselves how we can apply what we have learned to our continuing use of bodily action in the liturgy.

The group session can be closed with some thought on "where do we go from here?" This might be done personally, allowing each of us to choose how to heighten our bodily participation in the liturgy. It might also include a sharing of suggestions and resolutions to be passed on to the liturgy committee.

Those of us responsible for preparing and evaluating the liturgy will find we have more than enough feedback and ideas for application to take to our committee meetings.

PREPARATION AND EVALUATION

Caring for the body languages of liturgy is a responsibility we cannot afford to slight in preparing and evaluating liturgical celebrations. At times the preparation of text and song seems to claim our entire attention. Readers master words, but ad lib how they move to the lectern and stand there. Homilists prepare powerful lines about the importance of God's word, but neglect the message they communicate through an inattentive, slouching posture while that word is being proclaimed. Liturgy committees seek to engage the minds of the assembly with compelling themes of joy or repentance, but neglect to ask if those sentiments can be more powerfully evoked by engaging people's bodies.

The movements, postures, and gestures of the liturgy deserve our attention every time we prepare. This should not be taken to mean that we need to insert unusual things like dance or mime into every liturgy. Rather, the actions at stake are the ordinary actions called for in every liturgy. It is these that we must attend to, since they are a critical element in the total communication system of the celebration. I would like to suggest several important areas of concern for those who prepare the celebration.

First, in designing a celebration we should pay close attention to the typical kinds of liturgical actions that bear so much of the liturgy's meaning. Will kneeling for the penitential rite evoke a deeper sense of the meaning of the lenten season? How can we effectively use postures and gestures, such as standing and the raising of hands, to express our Easter joy? Can we engage the assembly more fully in processions with gifts, with hosanna palms? Memory of the impact of the processions on rogation days and Corpus Christi offers us a pastoral goal.

Second, the postures, gestures, and movements of the liturgical ministers deserve special attention. Even though the individual ministers are not always "on" during the liturgy, they are never out of sight of the assembly, and their bodies inevitably convey and model something for the assembly. How can we transform their movements, postures, and gestures, even the most utilitarian, into an integral part of what their roles say? Can we choreograph their actions into a visually pleasing corporate statement on mutual service in the assembly? Providing apt coaching and direction for ministers preparing to serve in the liturgy is something we owe the assembly.

Third, the preparation we provide for the ministers has to go beyond mere technical performance skills. We need to help them sense the inner feeling and unspoken meaning of their postures and gestures. This includes several things - a sense of reverence for the action as the depository of the community's sacred meanings, a sense of care for the full humanness of the action, a sense of the holiness of an action which becomes God's self-disclosure and self-gift to the people. It also includes helping them learn to do what all athletes and actors do, to "warm up" before the action begins. These are the things that turn the technical skills of the ministers into acts of prayer with the assembly.

Finally, in preparing the various actions of the celebration, we need to always think of them in terms of how and what they communicate to the assembly. Can the assembly see what happens? Can the assembly move in response? Will the action engage the bodily senses of the assembly and speak to them?

There are also a number of problem areas we might well note

as we make our preparations. One such problem is the way in which seating arrangements for the assembly may lock people in and deprive them of their ability to move or to see. Another problem we often face is an inherited mistrust of our bodies and a reluctance to let them be engaged in the liturgy, whether on the part of ministers or assembly. We also find it hard to overcome our compulsion to explain in words what every action and symbol should mean without giving them a chance to speak on their own. Alerting ourselves to these problems is a good beginning; in some cases it will take more concerted effort to overcome them.

Resources to help us in preparing the bodily actions of our celebrations are not as plentiful as we might hope.[6] But that may be to our benefit, since it forces us to look to our own experience and to on-the-spot help from people who have the skills to coach others in effective body movement and communication. In the end, we learn skills in body language not through reading about it, but through experience and practice under the tutelage of others. Live coaching is also more apt to help us develop our individual capacities than woodenly imitating what authors say we should do.

What qualities ought we look for in preparing and evaluating liturgical movements, postures, and gestures that communicate well? The following additions to the overall norms and qualities already suggested in the chapter on qualities and criteria seem pertinent.

Norm: Effective pastoral liturgy demands an uncommon sensitivity to the common gestures, movements, and postures required to wholly engage embodied persons in celebrating the presence of their God and their oneness as God's people (EACW #55).

Prepare and evaluate:

1. *Prayerful, unifying gestures.* Gestures should be full in both a visual and tactile sense and performed so as to foster prayer and unity in the assembly (EACW #56). Evaluation question: Did the gestures collect and embody the prayer of the assembly?

2. *Postures that engage and support.* The liturgy and liturgical space should be planned so as to enable the members of

the assembly to share the common postures required for their full participation and mutual support (EACW #57-58). Were members of the assembly enabled to participate in the celebration and support one another by means of bodily posture?

3. *Purposeful, graceful processions and movement.* The design of the celebration and the liturgical space should allow for processions and movement performed with purpose, grace, and confidence by ministers and members of the assembly (EACW #59). Were members of the assembly appropriately engaged in procession and movement?

Summary question: Was the liturgy fully embodied in movement, posture and gesture, especially by the liturgical ministers?

Notes

1. Some sources for this essay and for further readings are: Edmond Barbotin, *The Humanity of Man* (Maryknoll: Orbis Books, 1975), 187-224; Marianne Micks, *The Future Present. The Phenomenon of Christian Worship* (New York: Seabury, 1970), 18-34; Arthur A. Vogel, *Body Theology. God's Presence in Man's World* (New York: Harper & Row, 1973), 87-110; Joe Wise, *The Body at Liturgy* (Cincinnati: North American Liturgy Resources, 1975).

2. I experienced this forcefully several years ago when a group of new acquaintances identified, from my ways of acting, the exact area in Europe from which my ancestors had come five generations ago.

3. See *Assembly* 6 #3 (Dec. 1979) 73-80. This magazine is published by the Notre Dame Center for Pastoral Liturgy.

4. I wish to acknowledge the help Ralph Keifer, my colleague at CTU, has given me in developing this exercise.

5. I am indebted to Pat Shuckert, a free-lance liturgical dancer and dance therapist, for this exercise.

6. Some useful leads can be found in: Dennis J. Geaney and Dolly Sokol, *Parish Celebrations. A Reflective Guide for Liturgy Planning* (Mystic, CT: Twenty-Third Publications, 1983), 57-65; Gabe Huck, *Liturgy with Style and Grace* (Chicago: Liturgy Training Publications, 1984), 16-21; John P. Mossi (ed.), *Modern Liturgy. A Study and Planning Guide for Worship* (New York: Paulist Press, 1976), 153-177. There is more extensive literature on liturgical dance.

6

The Use of Liturgical Objects

THE TOPIC OF THIS CHAPTER, THE USE OF LITURGICAL OBJECTS, IS
limited in two ways. We will not have to treat liturgical action as
broadly as we did in the last chapter, where we covered liturgical
movement, posture, and gesture. Rather, we will consider only
those ritual actions that involve the use of objects. Nor will we
have to deal with the whole array of liturgical symbols, since
much has already been written about their origins, history, and
meaning. Rather, we will limit ourselves to those liturgical
objects used directly in ritual actions.

THE EXPERIENCE OF USING SYMBOLIC OBJECTS

Let's begin[1] with a nostalgic review of some of the typical
symbolic objects we hold dear as humans. The examples that
follow are chosen at random, and you are invited to add your
personal favorites to the list if they're not there and to spend a
little time re-living the situations these objects represent.

Perhaps the finest examples are the gifts we receive from or
give to people we love. Think of the care taken to choose just the
right gift, the moment of joy when it is handed over and
unwrapped, and the pleasure we take in using or displaying the
gift. Notice how saddened we are when a cherished gift wears
out, and how often we refuse to discard it even then.

Married and family life is filled with countless symbolic objects.
There are wedding rings and souvenir pieces of cake or clothing
from the wedding day. Nooks and crannies of our houses and

memories are filled with outgrown baby shoes, home-made birthday cards, and well-worn game boards. Chances are the dinner table was one of the first pieces of furniture purchased for the home. And then there are the special lace table cloth, candelabra, silver, and china that only make their appearance on certain occasions. And every kitchen has its share of stained, dog-eared recipes which identify the favorite foods of family and friends. Think of the story wrapped up in each of these things.

Is there any young adult for whom the keys to the family car are not a symbol of coming of age? Remember the long wait until we could take the driver's education program, the relentless pursuit of opportunities to drive under a parent's watchful eye, the first time the keys were handed to us and we were allowed to go it solo?

Or think of a graduation that marked an end and a beginning for us. The diploma a dean handed us and the tassel we moved to the other side of our "mortarboard" graduation cap soon ended up on our wall for all to see for years to come.

The occupations that are our daily grind provide their share of symbolic objects, too. We all have a favorite paring knife, a hammer without which we just can't work, or a cheap pen we refuse to give up for the better one in our drawer.

As we mull over the part these sorts of objects play in our lives, we begin to notice a number of common features that run through our examples.

It seems almost superfluous to note that the things we have named are all sensory objects, objects which appeal primarily to our senses of touch and sight. But notice how regularly we choose objects that are pleasing to the eye and hand. Even though the objects may be intended for utilitarian purposes, as in the case of our working tools, we still prefer those that have a pleasing quality and a human feel about them.

These objects do not take on their significance for us of themselves. They are all associated in one way or another with our human action at some significant moment. Think, for example, of the graduation tassel that hangs on a wall. At first it might seem insignificant. But remember that moment when we reached up and moved it from one side of our mortarboard to the other? The academic toil of long years was summed up in that simple movement. And so it is with all our examples. The objects find their meaning in their moment of use, when the gift is handed over, when we turn on the car's ignition, when we set the table and serve the favorite meal. But those are not isolated actions. Think of all the things we have done to prepare for that moment, all the time and effort that went into making or shopping for the right gift, the hours of coaxing and holding out a supporting hand before the child could walk alone, or the time spent planning and cooking the meal. Nor does the meaning of the object end with the moment of use. Think of how we display tassels and gifts and our best china. We want people to see and admire them, to touch them - with care! We keep important objects like special tools, family silver, and the sweater someone gave us safe and in repair, ready to use again. A whole history of human action is summed up in such symbolic objects. They are truly human objects.

As we reflect on those objects we are also struck by how constantly they are caught up in our human interactions. We hand the gift to a friend who accepts it from us. We cook the meal and serve it to our family for them to eat. Our parents teach us to drive and we take them to the store or the train. Just as our actions towards one another embody our mutual roles and relationships and communicate our shared values and feelings, so also do the objects we associate with those actions. They become the bearers of our bonds and our values. A ring is cherished because it sums up a relationship. A tattered recipe is kept in the recipe box because of our love for our family or friends. A favorite tool embodies our sense of the dignity and value of the work we do in service of others.

That, finally, is the meaning such objects have for us. They are the depositories of all the human acting and interacting that fashioned them, uses them, and keeps them. They bear the memory imprint of our human lives together, and they word-lessly renew our bonds and shared values whenever we touch them with hand or eye. In contrast, when we discard them they become relics and antiques that no longer speak our lives, except as dim reminders of the past. The objects we use and keep are sensory objects that have been taken from our physical world and transformed into living human symbols. They are the touch-stones of a larger process by which we constantly humanize our world and draw the things that fill it together into a texture and network of human meaning.

Against that background let us now turn to our experience of using liturgical symbols. As we did with our experience of using human objects, we'll begin with a nostalgic review of some of the liturgical objects we cherish. Feel free to add your own as we conjure them up.

Lighted candles are one of the most constant examples. We watch the Easter candle move in stately procession through the darkened assembly. We hold tapers in our hands. We hold our breath while a server who is a little too short tries to light the altar candles that are a little too high and we know that the service is ready to begin when the miracle is accomplished. We take a baptismal candle home and keep it safe until the child grows.

Or think of the lectionary carried in procession by a reader, raised aloft for an alleluia, enthroned on a lectern for the readings and for later veneration. The lectionary may be decorated with an artful cover that changes from season to season. The lectern itself is more than a crude ledge. It is elaborately made, adorned now with flowers, another time with an elegant draping.

It is not only lecterns and altars that we drape with fabric. Servants of the assembly, from usher to presider, are vested in their finest and in flowing garments as they minister to us, their roles of service cued for us by the symbolic garb they wear.

And there is the incense whose dancing tendrils of smoke curl upward in our sight and whose scent delights, or sometimes overpowers, our sense of smell.

But most of all there are the objects that focus the actions we call sacraments. A simple table is set with carefully chosen vessels. Bread and wine are brought forth, lifted up, divided, and shared. Water is blessed, sprinkled on our heads, poured with splashing sound into a font or pool where a people can be washed clean. Oils with soothing feel and penetrating scent balm the body.

As we dwell in the memory of these and other liturgical objects, we cannot help but notice the special qualities they share in their use.

They are all objects that touch the body in sensory fashion. We take care to give them a pleasing quality, so that they may truly awaken sight, touch, taste, and smell. We attend to the color, texture, and cut of vestments, to the scent of incense and oil, to the appearance and ingredients of the bread and wine. And to underscore the preciousness these objects have for us, we present them, serve them, and keep them in receptacles and furnishings which are themselves prepared with loving craft. Think of the care we invest in the form and feel of the vessels for the bread and wine, in the style and grace of candlesticks and stands for an Easter candle, in the crafting of lectern, altar, and font. We are not content with objects that are appropriate in a merely utilitarian way, we insist that they be beautifully and carefully crafted and have a proper liturgical feel.

These objects, however, do not attain liturgical significance in isolation. They find meaning in the moment of their use. We light the candles, carry them in procession, and by their flickering light sing of a Light entering our dark world. We anoint the body with oil. We trace the form of the cross on ourselves. We bathe someone in the waters of the font. And so it is with all our examples. The objects exist only to serve some liturgical action. But that action is only a peak moment in a series of actions. Think again of all the time and effort spent in designing and crafting those objects, of their long history of past liturgical service, of how we keep them on display or in readiness to be used again in a future celebration of the liturgy. A whole history of human caring for and acting out the liturgical rite is summed up in these symbols. They have become symbols that truly encapsule the meaning of the liturgy.

Note, too, how the symbolic power of these liturgical objects is built on their physical characteristics and on an underlying history of being used as human symbols. The bread we offer is the fruit of the earth and the work of human hands about to become the Bread of Life. Our prayers are to rise like the incense we burn to lift our spirits with its sweetness. Water, dealer of death and life in nature and in human affairs, becomes the icon of something deeper. The human caring signed forth in applying oil to an ailing body speaks of a strengthening and healing touch which reaches deep within.

As we reflect on our use of these objects in liturgical action, we come to see how they are caught up in a larger liturgical interaction. We break the blessed bread to share it with one another. But the action is more than a horizontal sharing of food and life between members of the assembly. We take the bread and say yes to the Body of Christ. We touch others with cleansing water and anoint them with oil, knowing in faith that it is Christ who brings to life and heals. The liturgical objects thus become the embodiment of our liturgical interaction in the assembly, an interaction in which the Lord has become a partner.

That, finally, is the meaning such liturgical objects bear for us. They are the depositories of all our liturgical interacting, they bear the memory imprint and promised fulfillment of all that we celebrate in the liturgy. They renew, without words, our bonds and shared values as God's people whenever we touch them with hand or eye. If we discard them, they are banished to reliquaries and museums as dim reminders of our past. But if we use them and keep them, they become the touchstones of what it means to live together as christians in our world.

What, then, does the experience of using liturgical objects tell us? It tells us that the objects we use as God's holy, embodied people are holy, too. It tells us that the world from which they are drawn is a holy, sacramental world. It tells us that the things of our world are not meant to be impenetrable barriers between God and us. It tells us, rather, that by God's creative design and power they are no more than thin veils which bring us near to the God they hide. If we care for the manner in which we use our liturgical objects, they become the keepsake symbols we use again and again to celebrate our journey as God's people.

CATECHESIS FOR LITURGY

Attending. The first step in the catechetical process we have been following is to attend to our experience. In doing catechesis on our experience of the use of liturgical objects it is especially important that we carry out this first step without taking any short cuts. In the case of some symbols we may already be so steeped in explanations of what the symbols ought to mean that we miss what our experience actually tells us. In other cases we may have the opposite problem, that of having no reflective awareness whatever of the symbolic objects we use or of what they mean. Our guiding question for this step is one we need to answer honestly. What do we actually experience when we use liturgical objects?

The first phase in attending to our experience is to recover it as a living experience. We can do this either by reminiscing about our past experience or by actually going through the experience.

The kinds of human experience cited in the first part of this chapter offer one possible topic for an exercise in reminiscing.

Our lives are filled with such special human objects and we have not been highly programmed as to what they should mean. When the group is gathered and ready to reflect, a leader can take us back to some shared arena of human activity, such as home and family life, and have us identify the special objects and recapture their significance. This might be done together as a group from the start, making use of descriptive questions. Our experience of liturgical objects presents a more challenging topic, for the two reasons given in the previous paragraph. It is possible to revive the experience through a reminiscing exercise, particularly if we focus on the symbols of a special season or sacramental celebration. Here, too, the reminiscing can be done together using descriptive questions.

An exercise in which we actually experience the use of liturgical objects is not hard to design and carry out. It has the decided advantage of helping us resolve the difficulties of too much or too little awareness of the experience and what it means, and it respects the non-verbal character of the "body knowing" which takes place in liturgical action.

Let me describe one such exercise a colleague and I have often used.[2] It requires several simple resources: a space that can be turned into a conducive setting, good examples of the liturgical objects to be used, one or more vested ministers who can rehearse their parts beforehand, and, if possible, some poetic reflections on the objects and actions in question. The reflections we have found most effective appeared in an issue of *Assembly* magazine which was devoted entirely to liturgical objects.[3]

For the exercise the group is best arranged in circular fashion. The exercise should be prayerful and well paced. It consists of a series of actions performed by the minister(s) using the pertinent liturgical objects. A reflective reading can precede or follow the action, depending on the emphasis desired, but the actions themselves are best done in silence. A longer exercise might include the use of: incense, candle, cross, water, oil, lectern, lectionary, table, tablecloth, plate and cup, bread and wine, and incense. The series might be shorter, focusing on objects for eucharist, baptism, or anointing. It helps to involve the group in silent actions to engage the senses of touch and sight (watching) as much as possible. For example, a minister facing a hand-held crucifix can silently mirror the outstretched form of the Crucified, sign herself or himself, and then hold the crucifix before each member of the group for them to repeat the signing gesture. Water that has been poured into a decorative bowl with the sound of splashing can be passed around the circle for participants to use in signing each other. A minister can anoint the palms of the participants with a nicely scented oil. The Gospel book can be taken around the circle for each to kiss, and so on. In each case, a minister models the action first, so that the participants need no prior instruction.

In the group discussion following the exercise people are asked to describe what they experienced. Do not neglect those who served as ministers. In facilitating this discussion the leader must be willing to spend time helping the people to give voice to what they actually experienced. It is important that the leader ask people to start by describing their sensory experience. This is the experiential, sacramental base for what the objects have to say to us.

At this stage in both reminiscing about and actually experiencing the use of liturgical objects the group can now be guided to the last phase of attending to their experience, that of naming the inner quality of what they felt. We will then be ready to move into the second step of the process.

Reflecting. The second step of the catechetical process we have been following is that of reflecting on our experience and that of others. What we seek to uncover in our reflection is the meaning the experience has for us and for our community.

Uncovering the meaning our own experience has flows easily from the previous step. After we have described our experience and named its inner feeling, the leader has us answer questions of meaning. What does the experience tell us about who we are as God's people, about how God meets us, about the value and dignity of our world, about our God? In answering these questions we open up the liturgical objects we use and come to see how they are symbolic statements about the larger meaning of our life and world. As we gather our answers to these questions of meaning, we need to raise the counter-question that helps us connect the outer experience of the symbolic objects and their inner meaning: Why? What is there about the experience that suggests that meaning to us? When the meaning of our own experience has begun to take on this larger shape, we are ready to hear what that experience has meant in our community's tradition.

First, the scriptures provide an abundance of materials on symbols such as water, light, food, and oil. One way to explore these might be to do some form of reading and shared reflection on how the passages speak to us. The human roots of these symbols in near-eastern culture should not be neglected.

Second, the history of our liturgical use of symbolic objects such as these is rich and easily accessible. We might ask a resource person to help us with a more difficult aspect of historical study, that of reading the story these objects tell of our ancient yet ever changing ways of following the Lord. To put it another way, we need someone to set the symbols in their human and social context at different periods of our history. This kind of contextualizing helps us understand how the use of our symbols has evolved in the course of time. That understanding is critical if we are to maintain a sense of fidelity to both the traditional liturgical use and the human roots of a symbol. When that sense of fidelity is lacking we easily reduce our symbolic objects to being either sacred relics from the past or pale contemporary human imitations of the powerful liturgical symbols they once were.

Third, section six of the U.S. Bishops' *Environment and Art in Catholic Worship* (EACW #84–106) outlines our church's contemporary outlook on the use of liturgical objects and provides worthwhile material for input and discussion.

Finally, a skilled, articulate liturgical artist or minister might be invited to help the group understand how a liturgical object is created or used.

The aim here is not to do an art history, but to help us set our experience within that of the larger community so that we are challenged to deepen and grow in our experience.

Applying. The third step of our catechetical process involves asking ourselves how we can apply what we have learned to our continuing celebration of the liturgy.

The concluding group discussions in the previous step, which bring our experience of using liturgical objects into creative dialogue with that of our larger community, open naturally into a concern for application.

The first kind of application the group can work on is how we ourselves can experience and respond to our liturgical objects on a deeper level. We might be encouraged to make both personal and collective resolutions.

The second kind of application is that proper to the liturgy

committee which commissions liturgical objects, prepares their
liturgical use, and evaluates whether they are used meaningfully
in our celebrations. A committee concerned for the liturgical
experience of its actual assembly will welcome suggestions the
group may want to pass on.

PREPARATION AND EVALUATION

Liturgical objects are part and parcel of many of the common,
central actions of the liturgy. Together with the whole array of
bodily actions they form the liturgy's language of action. It is for
that reason that liturgical objects, along with liturgical action,
need the constant care of a liturgy committee if we are to once
again fully embody our liturgy. It is to be hoped that our
committees will have within their ranks members who are keenly
sensitive to the language of symbols and eager to argue their
case. Several aspects of the use of liturgical objects deserve a
committee's special attention.

First, it is important that we keep our priorities straight. Our
primary concern must be for the *use* of the objects; the objects
themselves remain secondary. They are meant to serve the
liturgical action of the assembly and its ministers. They are
extensions of the action and get their meaning from it. But that is
also the measure of their importance. The objects, like a concrete
shorthand, do capture, sum up, and preserve the meaning of the
actions. One of our temptations as we prepare a celebration is to
think of liturgical objects in isolation from the action, as though
they are important in themselves. The three judgments recommended by the U.S. bishops in the case of liturgical music can help
us maintain the right perspective. An object may be artistically
and liturgically superb, but that is not enough. The pastoral
judgment demands that we be attentive to how we use the object.
The object must be one that our particular ministers and
congregation can use with human familiarity and prayerful grace
to tell our story.

Second, part of our pastoral responsibility is to provide the
objects necessary for the liturgy. Having a harried committee
member page through a liturgical catalogue at the last minute is
hardly sufficient. The bishops insist that all objects used in our
liturgical celebrations "should be designed or selected in consultation with experts in both liturgy and art" (EACW #84). This

requires adequate lead time, especially for more permanent liturgical objects. A regular review, and house cleaning, of our liturgical cupboards and store rooms should be part of the advance preparation for each season.

Third, our preparation must also include the actions that make use of those objects. It is especially important that the liturgical ministers whose actions are performed as a service to and in full view of the assembly be well prepared. There are two phases to this preparation. The first phase is part of the basic training we provide for ministers. That training must include performance skills in the use of liturgical objects. There is a difference between carrying a lectionary or the people's gifts as holy objects and treating them as so much baggage to be gotten from here to there. Setting the assembly's banquet table with fine cloth and precious vessels is not the same as putting a place mat and melmac dishes on a kitchen table. The second phase comes in the preparation of the actual celebration at hand. A rehearsal or walk-through with the ministers is advisable if skills are waning or if objects are to be used in a special way.

Fourth, we should also give thought to what happens to the objects in the aftermath of their use in the celebration. This isn't just a matter of storing and repairing objects so that they are ready to be used again. We have to ask ourselves which of our liturgical objects deserve to be prominently displayed between liturgical gatherings because they so graphically sum up our awareness of being God's people. The artistry and care we bestow on places of public repose for these objects enshrine them as lasting icons which greet our eyes when we gather and nestle in our memories when we are apart.

There are also a number of problem areas a liturgy committee needs to face in preparing the use of liturgical objects. One of these is our tendency to duplicate symbols, either because the symbol is so powerful or because it is growing weak. The bishops warn us against an overdose of symbols (EACW #86). Multiplying the number of crosses or imposing it on other objects as an ornament weakens the power of the sanctuary cross. A second problem, the bishops say, is our tendency "to 'make up' for weak primary symbols by secondary ones" (EACW #87). This can only draw the assembly's attention away from the actions the primary symbols were meant to focus. An attractive sheaf of wheat on a wall hanging will not rescue an anemic loaf of bread on the table.

A third problem is our tendency to overlay other symbolic objects with words, whether spoken or stitched on (EACW #85). We hope to strengthen the non-verbal message of the objects with such words; what we usually succeed in doing is to cast doubt on the ability of those objects to say anything in their own right.

In all our preparation and trouble-shooting in this area we need to always insist for ourselves that liturgical objects are to serve the actions in which they are used and the assembly who sees and touches them.

For that reason, our experience and that of the assembly remains our primary resource and last court of appeal. Other available resources[4] can be of great service, provided we keep our priorities straight.

What qualities ought we look for in preparing and evaluating our use of liturgical objects? Much has already been said in the chapter on qualities and criteria. Only a few things need be added here.

Norm: "Each [liturgical object] should be not only suitable for its purpose but also capable of making a visual or other sensory contribution to the beauty of the action" (EACW #84).

Prepare and evaluate:

1. *Symbols that communicate*. By their quality and design liturgical objects "speak of the importance of the ritual action"; by the way they are presented to the assembly they "speak well or ill of the deed in which the assembly is engaged" (EACW #97). Good pastoral liturgy must therefore be attentive to the language spoken by the objects we use. Evaluation question: What did the liturgical objects communicate by their design and use in the celebration?

2. *No duplication*. Good pastoral liturgy resists multiplying liturgical signs and objects lest the assembly's attention to them be lessened (EACW #86). Was there duplication in the use of symbols?

3. *Respect for primary symbols*. Good pastoral liturgy strives to enrich the celebration by strengthening its primary

symbols, rather than by supplanting them with strong secondary symbols (EACW #87). Were primary and secondary symbolic objects kept in proper proportion?

4. *No symbols on symbols.* Good pastoral liturgy resists the tendency "to place symbol upon symbol" or "to cover them with a heavy curtain of texts, words and commentary" (EACW #85, 94) lest the basic symbols be diminished. Did the celebration use the basic symbolic objects without overlaying them with other symbols and words?

Summary question: Were the liturgical objects so used as to serve the liturgical action and prayer of the assembly?

Notes

1. Less has been written on the experience of using symbols than on the symbols themselves. Some seminal ideas can be gleaned from the following: Edmond Barbotin, *The Humanity of Man* (Maryknoll: Orbis Books, 1975), 319–338, regarding food and meal; Laurence F. X. Brett, *Redeemed Creation. Sacramentals Today* (*Message of the Sacraments*, 8) (Wilmington: Michael Glazier, 1984), 78–97, 114–142; Joseph Gelineau, *The Liturgy Today and Tomorrow* (New York: Paulist Press, 1978), 95–103.

2. I owe this exercise to the inspiration and help of Kathleen Hughes, R.S.C.J., a CTU colleague.

3. *Assembly* 8 #1 (Sept. 1981) 137–144. This magazine is published by the Notre Dame Center for Pastoral Liturgy.

4. See, for example: The Bishops' Committee on the Liturgy and The Catholic University of America Center for Pastoral Liturgy (ed.), *The Environment for Worship: A Reader* (Washington, D.C.: USCC, 1980); Laurence F. X. Brett, *Redeemed Creation. Sacramentals Today* (*Message of the Sacraments*, 8) (Wilmington: Michael Glazier, 1984), 78–97, 114–142; Thomas G. Simons, *The Ministry of Liturgical Environment* (Collegeville: Liturgical Press, 1984), 21–37.

7

Liturgical Speech

WE TURN NOW TO THE FINAL LITURGICAL LANGUAGE, THAT OF speech. A few preliminary ideas on verbal language were sketched earlier, in the introduction to part two, to provide us with a model for the other liturgical languages. Full treatment of the topic has been reserved until now for a reason which I find most compelling and hope will become clear as these two chapters unfold. Liturgical speech does not stand alone. It has its fullest meaning only in the context of the entire liturgical event, when it names and sums up what all the liturgical languages wish to convey to us. This chapter will look at liturgical speech in a more general way; the following chapter will focus on that heightened form of speech we call song.

THE EXPERIENCE OF LITURGICAL SPEECH

It may seem strange to use the term 'speech' in the context of liturgy.[1] Why not a more familiar term like 'word' or 'language?' After all, we're accustomed to hearing about the "liturgy of the word" and the "language of prayer."

That last sentence already gives us a partial answer. Our purpose here is to think about the use of human speech in the liturgy in a larger way than those familiar phrases would suggest. The choice is also important because of what the different words convey to us about human speaking. In a literate culture like ours, where the vast majority of us is able to read and write and where books and newspapers abound, we tend to think of language as a system of writing which is meant to be read, though it may also happen to be pronounced on occasion. In a society like ours, which prides itself on collecting words in lexicons, defining them in dictionaries, processing them on computers, and scoring points by assembling them on scrabble boards, we tend to think of words as so many things out there which have isolated, exact meanings. But language is first and foremost a system of spoken communication. Words are meant to exist and find their full meaning in our act of speaking. It is our experience of the act of speaking in liturgical celebrations that concerns us here.

What is our human experience of speaking?

The physiology of it is simple enough. Air being expelled from the lungs (to dispose of carbon dioxide waste products) is pressed into one final service. We use it to set our vocal cords vibrating, thus producing sound which is further molded while still in our throats and finally shaped into words in our mouths. But that hardly scratches the surface of the mystery of human speaking.

It all began when we were babies, happily babbling away. Far from being just an amusing pastime, that babbling was a form of verbal scribbling. We were already at work sorting out sounds and ways to pattern them, learning from our parents which to discard and which to keep for later use. A mammoth task indeed for one so young! When we had mastered that repertoire of sounds, we were ready to speak our first words in our mother tongue.

That was indeed a proud moment for our doting parents, but only the beginning of a far more arduous and complex task. There was a whole new world around us filled with things and people now in need of names as we reached out to point to them or touch them. We started with names we could use to identify everything and everyone in our environment, by how they appear to us, by what they do, by how they relate to us (hot means that stoves burn, chairs are for sitting, and parents take care of us). We had begun to explore the meaning of that world by learning words about it.

From there it moved inexorably. Tenses, conjunctions, and prepositions gradually introduced us into the mysteries of temporal and spatial relations. The mental pictures that first filled our words did a slow dissolve into the ideas that let us get to the heart of things. Concrete, casual connections blossomed into an understanding of causes and consequences. We learned to store our growing set of words and all they represented in our memories and in writing, to be retrieved when we recognized familiar faces and facts and situations in our world, or to be pressed into service as creative new metaphors when we met something new and unfamiliar. As our language ability grew and enabled us to speak not only about the immediate, concrete, and specific but also about the more general, abstract, and remote, it swept us into an ever larger and more complex world, the world of our adulthood.

As we think back over the way our speaking has grown, we can begin to sense the magnitude of the mystery. It begins with our sensory impressions of the people and things of the world around us. But these impressions, channeled within us as nerve impulses and chemical reactions, are somehow transformed into an inner impression, a mental awareness of that world. It is as though that world itself has somehow entered our inner awareness, at first vaguely, then with increasing clarity and meaning as we find words for it. And in a marvelous reversal, the mental images and ideas we have used within ourselves to name that world and unravel its meaning find their way outward. We command our diaphragm to expel our breath and our throats and mouths to shape it into words, and we speak forth the word that was within. Learning to speak words lies at the heart of it. Speech accomplishes our thought within us and expresses it outwardly.

But it is not just that outer-world-become-inner-word that our speaking expresses. We, too, become the objects of our thought and speech. We can focus directly on ourselves and talk about our inner feelings, our ideas, our dreams. We also reveal ourselves indirectly whenever we talk about the world out there. No matter how objective and impartial our words may pretend to be in expressing ideas or imparting information, they say something about us as well. The objective world of which we speak is really the world as we perceive it. In giving directions to a lost stranger we implicitly affirm that we are knowledgeable and trustworthy. Unless we make them into facades to hide behind, our words on whatever topic express ourselves as well.

That leads us to one last piece needed to complete our description of our experience of speaking. We not only speak to express ourselves and our world. We also speak for someone to hear. Expression and communication are the twin functions of our speaking. Let's dwell on that a bit more.

The mystery of our hearing complements that of our speaking. Sound waves emitted by the mouth of the speaker strike the hearer's eardrum, setting in motion the chain of neural impulses and chemical reactions that are ultimately transformed into an inner understanding within the hearer. Bodily acts of speaking and hearing have opened a bridge over which our inner awareness, our inner words can be shared between our human spirits. Hearer and speaker change places, the flow of the verbal traffic reverses, and a conversation is underway.

The topic of our conversation can range far and wide, touching every phase of our experience of our world and ourselves. Neither of those subjects is ever really absent from our speaking. In scientific speech we strive to be as objective as possible, eliminating personal bias and subjective impressions as far as we can. But even then, scientists recognize, we cannot eliminate ourselves totally from the picture. We have chosen ways of seeing the world and interacting with it to produce our scientific results. On the other end of the spectrum lies literary speech, where the author's fully personal way of seeing the world is paramount. Poetic expressions, richly developed metaphors, fresh new images invite us to see the world as the author does. But unless it is all a game or a pretense, the author succeeds in casting the world in a totally new light, in showing us the heart of things as they are.

In between the extremes of scientific and literary speech we find our everyday speaking. We communicate all that is necessary to carry out our practical tasks, but we also reveal ourselves in the process. Think of how often we address each other by name, or of how the tone of a phone conversation changes when we learn the name of the other party whose voice we had not recognized. In giving our name we present ourselves to the other, even in the most pragmatic exchanges. In calling others by name, we summon them to be present to us as persons. In calling each other by name and in speaking with another about the world as we see it, we constantly disclose and offer ourselves. If the other truly hears and accepts this self-expression, even while we talk about other things, the human communication is complete. Our speaking has bonded us together.

At this point it may be helpful to step back from our description and draw out a number of reflections about our experience of speaking.

First, there are many ways in which our speaking is framed. Words are framed by other words. Our experience of not being able to distinguish the flow of sound into words when we first begin to learn a foreign language confirms that. The words we have strung together into sentences and paragraphs as we converse are framed by what someone says before and after. The whole conversation is framed by words of greeting and parting.

There is a still more fundamental, less noticed framing that takes place. All speech is framed by silence. There is silence before the speaking begins and after it ends. The pauses between words and sentences, no matter how slight, are also a form of silence. But the human experience of silence goes far deeper than a physical silence that is the mere absence of sound. There is the silence of things that cannot yet be spoken, of feelings that cannot yet be named, of relationships not yet formed. There is the silence of speech fulfilled, when everything has been said, when our words have become too meager a communing. These, in turn, suggest that there must be a silence within our speaking, an inner stillness out of which speaking is born and to which it must return. Speaking that would be more than idle chatter, a form of noisy silence, must ultimately acknowledge that our words do no more than dimly reflect the mystery of the world and our persons, a mystery which always escapes them in the end.

Second, speaking goes hand in hand with acting. Our bodies are seldom still when we speak, setting up the multi-channel communication we spoke of earlier. We interpret our deeds in words. We substantiate our words with deeds. We've all heard the challenge, "put your money where your mouth is." The interconnection goes even further. We have already suggested that actions speak in their own way. Now we must add that speaking is a form of acting. Speaking commits us to what we know, to what we say. That is why solemn forms of speaking like oaths, declarations, contracts, and promises accomplish things and bind us. We have given our word.

Third, our human family has been far more successful in learning to deliberately preserve speech than we have with any other form of bodily language. That is one of the reasons why we see it as such a preeminent form of communication. Smells linger briefly; taste leaves only a fleeting aftertaste; touch quickly becomes a memory. Actions can be kept alive only in the objects they produce, in the continuing consequences and chain reactions they have set in motion, or in ritual repetition. Sight offers more possibility. We carve, paint, or photograph images we wish to keep before our gaze. And we have pressed that sense of sight into serving our speaking, first alongside oral tradition and then to supplant it. Over the course of centuries we first devised picture language and then more abstract, phonetic forms of written language such as our alphabet. And most recently we have found ways to preserve the spoken sounds themselves. What this means is that our speech can be lifted from its living context and preserved to be transmitted across space and time, for as long as its written and recorded traces survive.

This is a mixed blessing for us. We have gained an ability to "converse" with others of our kind across far reaches of space and time, giving ourselves access to people and worlds we would not otherwise know. But in that very process we have learned to reduce living speech to a residue of words which often leave us too little trace of the living mystery they were meant to disclose and convey. In a similar vein, we shape our living words to say uniquely what we wish to say. Recorded language takes on its own independent existence. From early on, for better or for worse, we are shaped by the words we learn from others. The language we learn shapes how we experience our world and ourselves.

Fourth, speech has given us a unique human power, a power no other bodily language can match with so little expenditure of energy. We know in our bones how important naming and being named are. Have you ever balked at giving your name over the phone to a stranger until you know what the person wants? Naming identifies us and gives another access to and power over us. Our ability to speak also contributes in a unique way to our human mastery over and creative shaping of the world around us. We capture the world in words. We then work with our words, refining them and creatively re-arranging them as a prelude to re-ordering the world itself. Isn't that what happens in any planning process? A similar process happens as we record and retell our human stories. They are realigned and reshaped into new meaning with each retelling.

This unique ability we have to shape words that stand for but exist apart from our world and to mold and reshape them leads us one step further. We use our words to talk about talking itself.

Such a meta-language is only minimally possible with other body languages, for example when we mimic or parody our actions. This enables us to nuance, clarify, and modify spoken communication to an amazing degree. It also enables us to create those rarified forms of abstract, logical language that seem so far removed from their birthplace in our actual experience of the world around us.

Fifth, the fact that we can detach our words and preserve them, leaving behind the original speaker, hearer, and discourse situation, has created a form of communication unique to speech. We can entrust a message to the memory of a messenger, to be delivered as living communication at a later time to someone who is absent. An author can commit a poem or a play to writing, leaving it to performers to transform into living words for some future audience. But note what happens in this process. The words that are the residue of the living speech and self-expression of their author must be brought back to life in the mouth of an actor or an oral interpreter. This process is not simply a matter of sounding, or mouthing the words on the page. The words come alive only if they are made to resonate with the experience that first gave rise to them. Depending on the type of material at hand, performers have several ways of transforming the words into living speech. They can recreate the experience for hearers by dramatizing the character portrayed, by infusing the words with similar experience of their own, or by telling the words in story fashion. Note, too, how this requires messengers and actors to leave behind their own personal words to enter into the words of another. This form of speaking is nearest to the speech we experience in liturgical celebration.

What, then, is our experience of liturgical speech?

Let's begin by listing the kinds of speech we experience in the liturgy. Speaking occurs not only in the liturgy of the word, but throughout every part of the celebration. There are: presidential prayers to which we respond with amens and acclamations; readings with responses; homilies; prayers said in unison by all (such as the confiteor, creed, and Lord's prayer) and prayers said in dialogue (such as ritual greetings, invitations to prayer, litanies, and responsorials).

As we mull over these forms of liturgical speaking, several unique things begin to stand out.

First, one of the unique things about liturgical speech, unlike our ordinary human conversation, is that our words in the liturgy are almost all scripted in advance. Think of how startled we are when a liturgical minister departs from the text, or how at a loss for words we feel when the presider changes the words of a ritual greeting. The words we read and hear, the prayers we say, even the greetings we exchange are words given to us by others. The readings are God's word. Liturgical theology tells us that it is God who speaks when the scriptures are read in the assembly. Our ritual exchange of words at the conclusion of the reading say it more simply. "The Word of the Lord. Thanks be to God." The words we say and hear in our prayers and dialogues are given to us by the christian community. Even the homily, with its freedom of expression, is to flow out of the readings and to content itself with breaking open their meaning for our lives.

This places some unique demands on liturgical speech. Texts have to become living speech, filled with the stuff of our experience as God's people. We recognize immediately when a reader or prayer leader utters them as so many fossilized words devoid of the breath of life. And all of us, presiders, readers, and assembly alike, face the challenge of laying aside our own words and allowing ourselves and the inner meaning of our lives to be named and shaped by the words given us by our God and our community.

Second, a marvelous pattern begins to emerge if we step back from the words we speak in the liturgy and look at their content. The scripture readings are a unique form of literature. Together they form an epic story which witnesses in awe and humble faith to God's earthly presence to us in all the seemingly ordinary and out of the way experiences of life. Close examination shows that this same sense of story pervades all our public liturgical prayers. After addressing God, we always devote the first part of those prayers to remembering and telling, with praise and awe, the story of God's past dealings with us. And in the second part of the prayer, strengthened by that memory, we look to the future and plead with God to aid us in our need and to continue to accompany us on the journey that lies ahead. Our response to the story told in the readings and broken open in the homily is similar, though more extended. We are led from thanks and praise in our initial responses, to a meditative re-living in psalm and silence, to believing acceptance in creed, and to supplication and yearning in prayers of intercession.

This larger pattern tells us that there is a larger story to our lives than their daily bits and pieces can tell, a meaning that runs deeper than the surface appearances. We are challenged to speak the words of the liturgy in such fashion that we hear our story and voice our need.

Third, it is striking to what an extent liturgical speaking takes the form of a dialogue involving the entire assembly. There is to be no audience in liturgy. Even lengthy readings and prayers receive a response, since they are addressed to the assembly or spoken in its name.

But if we look more closely at the liturgical dialogue, we'll see that it takes several different concrete forms: words said by a spokesperson, words said in unison, and words said in alternating ritual dialogue. Each of these forms tells us something different about who we are as an assembly. The experience of praying in unison tells us that we are all full and equal members of the assembly, that the liturgy is ours to do. The experience of the various forms of ritual dialogue tells us that we are to support each other in the prayer we share. The experience of readers who speak to us in God's name and of leaders who pray to God in our name tells us that we accept and say amen to differing roles of service in our community. Above all, that experience tells us that God has become a partner, both speaker and listener, in the dialogue that takes place in our assembly.

Fourth, our liturgical speaking always goes hand in hand with the ritual actions, gestures, and postures explored in an earlier chapter. We stand, kneel, and raise our hands to pray. We stand to proclaim and sit to listen. We touch and bathe and feed one another to the sound of words. Liturgical speaking is never an isolated communication.

What this says to us is that the meanings of speech and action are to merge. As in human communication, we most readily believe those words which name what we actually experience. The power of such words lies precisely in their ability to draw the inner meaning of our experience to the surface of our awareness and to name it. We are easily put off by words which belie our actions or which are hollowed out of all experience. Such words are idle liturgical chatter.

Fifth, liturgical speaking easily suffers the same fate as our everyday words, that of selective hearing. Whether it is due to our cultural conditioning, the very repetitiousness of ritual itself, or our experience of a liturgy in which the words are too many, too prosaic, and too poorly spoken, selective hearing remains a fact of our liturgical experience. We can easily check that out by trying to jot down all the words we remember from last Sunday's liturgy, for example. Chances are we will come up with no more than a few phrases. Or think of how rote the ritual dialogues become. "... And also with you ... We lift them up to the Lord." We can rattle off the words in our sleep.

This suggests several questions. May not the importance of the ritual dialogues lie less in what is said than in the fact that they engage us mutually at critical points in the celebration? Or might they not function as a kind of mantra meant to lead us to a stillness within? Or think again of the phrases we are able to dredge up from our Sunday celebration. Don't they tend to be strong images, metaphors, or poetic turns of phrase that resonate with our lives? Might not the power of our words lie less in rational discourse than in the intuitive naming of our lives, our relationships, our world in new ways?

Sixth, liturgical speaking, like all human speaking, at some point needs to be framed in silence. If we listen attentively to what is happening on the liturgical scene, we increasingly hear people call for and tell of the restoration of more silence in our liturgies.

What intuition lies behind this? Is it not our sense that God is, finally, one whom we cannot name or comprehend? And if we are made in God's image, are we not also an unspeakable mystery to ourselves, when all is said and done? We experience liturgical speaking at its best when it is couched in a reverent silence, a stillness which precedes, fills, and follows all our words.

What, then, is the message of our liturgical speaking? It tells us that we are a people in dialogue with God, bonded to God and each other in the words we speak and the story we tell. It names us to God and to each other. It names and shapes the inner meaning of our life journey in our world.

CATECHESIS FOR LITURGY

Attending. The task of catechizing ourselves on the experience of liturgical speech begins by asking what we actually experience.

There are two ways in which we might go about recovering the experience by some form of reminiscing. The first approach is to begin by recalling the words and phrases that have made a deep and lasting impression on us. This can be readily done in full group discussion. The second approach, set in a reflective atmosphere, is to do reflective readings on some of the verbal formulas that occur again and again in our liturgical celebrations. Reflections of this type appeared in an issue of *Assembly* magazine devoted to ritual dialogue. [2]

The experience can also be recovered by means of several kinds of exercise. The very nature of speech suggests that a live experience works far better than just reminiscing about speaking, provided we can overcome the danger of too self-conscious a performance. A session with a professional storyteller or with literary readings by oral interpreters, if such resource persons are available in the locality, can be very effective in evoking an experience of the power words have for us. A parallel, explicitly liturgical experience can be built around the use of prayers in a quiet setting. Similarly, the group might actually celebrate the liturgy of the word in one or more styles. It is important that such liturgical events be experienced as true prayer, not as demonstrations.

Once the participants have recovered their experience in either of these ways, they are ready to describe it. Descriptive questions put to the group by the leader should focus on uncovering the words, phrases, and images that struck people. Non-verbal elements, whether behavioral or environmental, can also be included.

Description of the experience of speech easily leads into our naming of the inner quality of the experience. Words are born to give voice to inner experience. Naming and descriptive questions are hard to keep apart in this case and might well be intertwined, provided the description is not neglected.

Reflecting. The second phase of the catechetical task asks what our experience of liturgical speaking means.

If we take up the experience we have been attending to as a group, the leader can help us put our experiences together into a larger, shared whole. It is at this point that some of the special characteristics of speech, which we noted in the essay above, will begin to surface. For example, if we use language to name the inner meaning of our life experiences and of our relationships to one another, it should be possible for us to trace back from the words to those inner feelings. The questions to ask are already familiar. What does our speaking in liturgy tell us about God, about being God's people, about our mutual bonds and roles? Our first tendency will be to look to the content of prayers and texts. We cannot afford to neglect the less obvious, but critically important contribution made by such things as the forms and patterns of our speaking in the assembly as we seek to answer these questions of meaning. The follow-up question will help us in that regard: Why? What is there about our ways of speaking in the assembly that enables them to convey that meaning?

As this larger sense of meaning comes together for the group, we are ready to turn to resource persons for what liturgical speech has meant to our community in the past.

First, an obvious area to turn to in scripture is what the bible tells us about the word of God. There are many beautiful texts and images to consider, such as the parable of the seed, the power of the word as a two-edged sword, the dew-like gentleness and fertility of the word, the biblical identification of word and event, and so on. In another vein, we might look to the way in which the celebration of the word developed in Judaism and the early church.[3]

Second, a simple sketch of the development of the liturgy of the word in liturgical history can be given.[4] The presenter should be careful not to overburden people with historical detail, but rather to sketch the developments from the standpoint of the assembly's role and involvement and to capture the flavor of the ups and downs of our community's long and varied experience of proclaiming the word of God and responding to it. Toward that end we might consider doing a more anecdotal account, drawing on such ancient accounts as that of the *Apostolic Tradition* of Hippolytus.

Third, current church perspectives on the liturgy of the word can be gleaned from the revised *Introduction to the Lectionary for Mass*.[5] The experience of church groups, such as the "base communities" in hispanic cultures, which meet regularly to share and reflect on the word of God, can also offer us some fresh perspectives from the larger christian community.

Fourth, if we have enlisted the help of oral interpreters or storytellers in the first step of our catechesis, we might ask them to lead the group in discussing the experience of bringing story and text to life.

With this material under our belts the group can return to discussion, to set our experience within that of the larger community.

Applying. The final phase of the catechetical task is to ask ourselves how what we have learned applies to our celebration of the liturgy.

The wrap-up discussion can help the group focus on potential areas of application and might well include suggestion box entries for the liturgy committee to take up in its work of preparing and evaluating our ways of speaking in the assembly.

PREPARATION AND EVALUATION

There are several important considerations for a committee to keep in mind as we prepare the spoken elements of the celebration.

It is often suggested, and rightly so, that the scripture readings assigned for the celebration are the place to start. However, our best approach to the readings is not to start by asking what their theme is. Rather, we should begin with a reflective reading of the passages, first asking ourselves what words, images, or moods catch our attention and resonate with what we and our local community are experiencing. The texts are destined to become live speech in the assembly, and the strength of the spoken word lies in its ability to name and express our experience. This way of starting our preparation process respects the nature of human speaking and sets us off on the right track.

The committee will be equally concerned to care for the way in which the texts are prayed and proclaimed by liturgical ministers. The challenge for these ministers is the same challenge actors and oral interpreters face, that of capturing the inner form of the written words, making it their own, and re-embodying it in the outer words they speak.[6] Practically speaking, the committee is usually in the best position to carry out the pastoral responsibility of making sure that all ministers of word and prayer speak together in harmony in the assembly. There are two specific services the liturgy committee owes the readers for the sake of the assembly. The first is to provide prospective lectors with adequate training in oral interpretation. The second is to work with those who will proclaim the scriptures at the liturgy being prepared. The readers and the committee need to work together to plan what they wish the readings to say and to ensure adequate rehearsal. The committee also needs to be in close communication with the presider-homilist and might well be represented on the homily preparation group recommended by the NCCB.[7]

In caring for the quality of whatever prayers or introductions we may need to compose for the liturgy, the committee should strive for a style that is figurative, evocative, and lean. We can only hope that the day of introducing the liturgy with lengthy statements of theme and prefacing the readings with a synopsis that excuses us from listening is rapidly coming to a close.

In preparing the celebration we also need to be much more attentive to restoring an effective use of silence to our celebrations. The silence we seek is not a momentary absence of physical noise and outer words, but rather that inner stillness that fills our words and centers our prayer.

Finally, we must also attend to the interplay of word and action, to make sure that they are saying the same thing, that our words actually name the meaning our actions do.

There are also a number of problem areas we would do well to keep in mind as we prepare: our tendency to rely too heavily on words which the assembly will only hear selectively, our compulsion to insert needless explanations, our tendency to think of liturgy as text rather than as live event which includes speaking, and the unjust exclusions our use of language so subtly works in the assembly. Forewarned is forearmed!

There is no dearth of pastoral resources in this area, a testimony to the amount of care expended on it since the liturgical renewal began.[8] The assembly's experience of liturgical speaking that truly engages them in dialogue remains our most critical pastoral resource in preparing how we use the word in worship.

What qualities ought we look for in preparing and evaluating our liturgical speech? The following ideas are meant to supplement what has already been said in the chapter on qualities and criteria.

Norm: "To promote active participation, the people
should be encouraged to take part by means of
acclamations, responses, psalmody, antiphons, and songs,

as well as by actions, gestures, and bearing. And at the proper times all should observe a reverent silence" (CSL #30 [DOL #30]).

Prepare and evaluate:

1. *Full liturgical dialogue.* In good pastoral liturgy a simultaneous dialogue takes place on two levels, between God and the people and between the gathered people and their ministers; that dialogue is summed up in the Amen of Christ, our mediator (ILM #6; GIRM #14 [DOL #1404]). Evaluation question: Was there a full liturgical dialogue?

2. *Mutual ministry through living speech.* Good pastoral liturgy requires that people and ministers embody liturgical texts in living speech, in mutual service of their common prayer (ILM #38-57; GIRM #18 [DOL #1408]). Did members of the assembly, especially presiders and lectors, effectively minister word and life to one another?

3. *Harmony between words and deeds.* In good pastoral celebrations words are spoken so that their meaning is in harmony with that of the liturgical actions. Did the meaning of words and deeds match?

4. *Times of silence.* Good pastoral liturgy frames speaking with times of reverent silence (ILM #28; GIRM #23 [DOL #1413]). Was there reverent silence?

Summary question: Did the assembly truly speak with God and one another in praise and prayer?

Notes

1. Some resources on which I have relied in preparing this reflection and which the reader might want to sample include: Edmond Barbotin, *The Humanity of Man* (Maryknoll: Orbis Books, 1975), 139–186; Joseph Gelineau, *The Liturgy Today and Tomorrow* (New York: Paulist Press, 1978), 75–81, 104–113; Georges Gusdorf, *Speaking (La Parole)* (Evanston: Northwestern University Press, 1965), translated by Paul T. Brockelman; Kathleen Hughes, R.S.C.J., *The Language of the Liturgy: Some Theoretical and Practical Implications (Occasional Paper [#2])* (Washington,

D.C.: International Commission on English in the Liturgy, 1984); Marianne Micks, *The Future Present. The Phenomenon of Christian Worship* (New York: Seabury Press, 1970), 54–85.

2. See *Assembly* 7 #3 (Feb. 1981) 113–120.

3. See Lucien Deiss, *God's Word and God's People* (Collegeville: Liturgical Press, 1976).

4. For some general overviews see: Johannes Emminghaus, *The Eucharist: Essence, Form, Celebration* (Collegeville: Liturgical Press, 1978); Robert E. Webber, *Worship Old and New* (Grand Rapids: Zondervan, 1982), 175–183; James F. White, *Introduction to Christian Worship* (Nashville: Abingdon, 1980), 110–144.

5. For text and commentary, see Ralph A. Keifer, *To Hear and Proclaim. Introduction: Lectionary for Mass. With Commentary for Musicians and Priests* (Washington, D.C.: National Association of Pastoral Musicians, 1983).

6. See James A. Wallace, *The Ministry of Lectors* (Collegeville: Liturgical Press, 1981), 15–18.

7. See The Bishops' Committee on Priestly Life and Ministry, *Fulfilled in Your Hearing. The Homily in the Sunday Assembly* (Washington, D.C.: USCC, 1982), 36–38.

8. In addition to the works of The Bishops' Committee on Priestly Life and Ministry, Ralph Keifer, and James Wallace cited earlier, a sample might include: *Celebrating Liturgy* (Chicago: Liturgy Training Publications, 1981–1983); Dennis J. Geaney and Dolly Sokol, *Parish Celebrations. A Reflective Guide for Liturgy Planning* (Mystic, CT: Twenty-Third Publications, 1983), 94–116; Gabe Huck, *Liturgy with Style and Grace* (Chicago: Liturgy Training Program, 1984), 76–81; Ray Lonergan, *A Well-Trained Tongue. Workbook for Proclaimers* (Chicago: Liturgy Training Publications, 1982); Mark Searle, *Liturgy Made Simple* (Collegeville: Liturgical Press, 1981), 33–52.

8

Liturgical Song

THIS FINAL CHAPTER WILL FOCUS ON THE LITURGICAL EXPERI-
ence of that heightened form of speech called song. We will
not be concerned, then, with the broader topic of liturgical music
or with questions of theory and techniques of performance.

THE EXPERIENCE OF LITURGICAL SONG

Our lives are filled with songs,[1] from the lullaby whose
metronome is the rocking of the baby's cradle to the sorrowing
song whose muffled beat marks time for the grieving of
mourners. Campfire songs and sing-alongs, kindergarten ditties
and high school fight songs, current entries in the top forty, folk
songs and songs from "our" time, songs for a broadway musical
and songs to sing in the shower, operas and great choral works of
art, little tunes we sing to ourselves when happy or sad - there's
hardly a time or situation in life in which we do not put our words
into music.

It is something we accomplish simply enough. We hold the
sound of a syllable for a certain time without gliding up or down
and create pitch and note. As our syllables and words flow on we
rhythmically add notes on different pitches and create a melody.
Our song is on its way. We fashion solemn pronouncements into
chants, the wisdom of our people into folksongs, our stories into
ballads, and our sorrows into dirges. We add the harmony of
many voices and sing in chorus. We refine our skills and our
ability to match words to sound and transform poems into art

songs, drama into opera, prayer into a chorale. We learn our songs, hand them on, and write them down, and soon our repertoire is bulging with a whole spectrum of folk, popular, and art songs.

On closer reflection we begin to notice that there is something special about our human experience of singing our songs. Song is a special kind of speaking. It is heightened speech. But it is not just the physical sounds of our words that are intensified. We are most prone to sing in times of joy and sorrow, when we fall in love, when we need to tell the stories that reaffirm who we are. We intensify the sound of our words to heighten the inner meaning they express. That is why songs are so adept at expressing the feelings and moods that grip us at those moments. And once we have learned the inner feeling of our songs, they evoke it in us again and again, whenever we sing them.

We also discover in our reflection how deeply our songs are embedded in the fabric of our relationships with others. They enrich and heighten our communication with each other. This is particularly true of the songs we sing together, around a campfire, at a pep rally, around the family piano, and especially during our gatherings for a feast. We sing the words and notes of the song together, our voices adopt the same pitch and pace and blend into one. Our very act of singing is an act of attending to one another.

But there is yet more to it. Song heightens the meaning our words bear for us. Shared song simultaneously evokes the same sense of meaning, the same feelings, the same sense of purpose in us. Think of the impact a marching song has on the participants in a rally. Or think of how certain songs burst into popularity because they have somehow caught and voiced the unexpressed mood of the times. Songs bond us in what we experience.

Because they are such effective expressions of the meaning of our lives together, songs easily take on larger, symbolic roles for us. The old songs evoke the old times and renew our bonds at a class reunion. Songs we shared with special friends in special moments become keepsakes for us. And if a radio station wants to capture our age bracket as a listening audience, they play our songs. Songs bridge our shared history.

What this line of reflection suggests to us is that singing is a unique language. But it raises a question. Is song only verbal language which happens to be set to music, or does the music add something new? Or to put it another way, is a song's meaning simply that of the spoken words with musical underlining and stress markers added, or does the singing contribute a meaning of its own? Experts are by no means agreed on how to answer this question, yet they voice several common themes which our experience seems to bear out.

One such theme is that music is somehow a common language that borders on being "universal." For example, children around the world use the same "na na, na na, na na" melody to tease one another. What this illustration suggests is that intervals based on the laws of harmonics seem to strike a common resonance in us. Sounds can become music capable of expressing something to us and we are born with a capacity to respond to that music.

But if music is a language, it is a language of metaphors, not of literal meanings.[2] We need only compare our musical taste with that of others to see how difficult it is to establish hard and fast meanings in the music we hear. Rather, like verbal metaphors, music gives us a way to name and express the inner quality of our experience as we live and interact in our world. Certain features of the music, such as dissonance, tempo, and unresolved chords may suggest similar feelings to us; but our responses may also vary widely. What this suggests is that music has its own intrinsic meaning, which we then associate with personal memories, inner states, and images evoked by our other life experiences. The musical expression serves as a metaphor for our experiences, setting its meaning alongside theirs in free, creative association.

From that point of view music acts very much like the language we call poetry. This is illustrated very graphically in the case of song which weds music to words, often words of poetry. If the words and the music are well matched, both will evoke, express, and communicate the same meaning in their own way. Neither is reduced to being a literal, slavish imitation of the other. Both are full partners, analogies for each other. Something similar might be said for the combination of music and action, as in a grand entrance march, for example. Action and music each point to the same human experience.

One final thing needs to be added about the uniqueness of the language of song. It not only intensifies speech, it has a power to name what words cannot, to express and communicate our experience in a way that is beyond the power of words alone. That is why we turn to song so naturally in times of joyful feast, holy awe, and deep sorrow.

Against that brief background, let us take up our experience of liturgical song.

Our liturgical experience of song has undergone radical change in the last several decades. Many of us can still remember the days when the "low mass," devoid of all singing, was the normal experience. There was usually one "high mass" each Sunday, at which priest and choir sang while we listened. If the common parts, such as the *Kyrie* and *Sanctus*, were being sung in gregorian chant and we felt brave, we joined in quietly.

In the years just before the Vatican Council we felt the first winds of liturgical change. A "dialogue mass" was introduced to allow some measure of congregational participation, albeit in Latin. Vernacular hymns sung by the congregation made their appearance as well. But notice where we sang them - at the beginning and the end of the liturgy and at the seams between its major parts. That "four hymn" practice tenaciously survives in many places.

Two decades ago the liturgical renewal touched off some major advances and changes in our singing patterns. A comparison of our present experience with that of the days of the "low" and "high" masses is instructive. By contrast, the presider does very little singing now, and choirs may either be non-existent or play a sharply reduced role. Rather, the bulk of the singing is now done by the assembly, supported by instrumentalists and led by cantor or small choral group. When choirs do sing, it is usually in support of or in musical dialogue with the assembly. Think, too, of when and what we sing. The motets and hymns in the seams have lost their pride of place to the responses and acclamations we sing during the liturgy of the word and the great eucharistic prayer.

If we look more closely at our current experience of liturgical singing, several things begin to stand out for us.

First, though there is occasional use of instrumental music, our liturgical music has become predominantly song. As we noted above, singing is a harmonious blend of speech and music in which each contributes uniquely to the total expression of what we are experiencing.

What this implies is that the musical component does not exist for its own sake, but as a partner to word in the liturgical song's total communication. Music's task is to intensify and enhance the meaning of the words in a way they cannot do alone. This partnership is being taken more and more seriously. We are learning from sad experience that both trite music and uninspired lyrics can rob song of its power to lift our hearts and voices. The artistic quality of both text and music is receiving increasing care and attention. Composers have also become more aware that various texts of the liturgy communicate in different ways and must be set to music that is correspondingly nuanced and varied. Ancient musical forms are being recovered and new ones created. Think, for example, of the music of Taizé or the creative new musical settings for the eucharistic prayer.

Second, we have experienced a union of song and action in the restored processions, for example. Most importantly, our singing has migrated from the edges and seams of liturgy back into the center of the action itself. The first priorities for singing are our responses during the liturgy of the word and our acclamations during the eucharistic prayer.

A new conception of the liturgical role of song begins to emerge as it moves to the center of the celebration. Liturgical song does not exist for itself, but to serve the central actions of the liturgy. Singing is more than a mere decoration or optional ornamentation. It is meant to be a true partner of speech and action in a full, multi-channel communication, with a unique contribution to make. What is that unique contribution? Song carries speech beyond itself to the point of stillness before the mystery that cannot be named or spoken. Song heightens and intensifies the meaning our actions have for us, just as it does with word.

At this point we might pause to note that unworded music is beginning to find a new role in liturgical celebrations parallel to that described for worded music in the last few paragraphs. Like worded music, it is being used to serve the assembly in a number of ways: to set an environment for the celebration, to frame and create movement, to intensify oral and reflective prayer, and to provide an avenue of expression for feelings too strong and deep to be put into words.

Third, our liturgical singing has been freed from its more rigid patterning to assume its more natural role in helping us mark our feasts and seasons with varying degrees of solemnity. We have learned to rely on the style and amount of singing we use to key our sense of celebration, varying from ordinary, standard liturgies to those times of high feast. In this fashion we have simply extended singing's ability to intensify the meaning of words and actions to include feasts and seasons.

Fourth, restoration of full participation of the assembly in liturgical celebration has led us to include several different forms of singing. Though we still occasionally find ourselves listening to works performed for the assembly by choirs or soloists, the new liturgy clearly prefers that the assembly not be reduced to being a passive audience. Unison songs by the whole assembly and dialogic songs in which assembly responds to minister, cantor, or choir now predominate.

If we stop and think about it, each of these forms implies a different ecclesiology of the assembly.[3] Songs performed by choir or soloist stress hierarchical roles. Congregational songs sung in unison speak of the importance and self-sufficiency of the assembly. Songs with a dialogic form imply a theology of the assembly in which both the full equality of all and the ministerial roles of particular members are important. These same implications might be drawn in a larger way from the whole set of songs used in a liturgical celebration.

Fifth, restoration of the full participation of the assembly in liturgical singing has also made an impact on the style of our singing. When we relied primarily on ministers and choir to do the singing, it was feasible to insist on more professional training and preparation and to use forms of music that were technically more demanding. Musical forms were more formal and classical. Performance was marked by a sense of precision and a more studied expression. As the assembly at large has been brought more and more into the singing, there has been a shift to forms of music more akin to folk and popular styles. The demand placed on liturgical music now is that it be singable, in terms of range, melody, and degree of elaboration. Musical forms tend to be more simple; spontaneity of expression and lack of musical self-awareness often characterize the singing. In that light it is not surprising that we have had to struggle with tensions and differences of opinion, often cast as "folk" versus "sacred" music.

What message, then, does our experience of liturgical singing convey to us? Its message is not a different one than that spoken to us by word and action. Rather, it intensifies the message and, like silence, sustains the meaning when we reach that moment when our words must become mute, when our deeds must be stilled. If we truly sing, we do not just sing the message of the words; we sing the song "until it is all sung out and there is nothing left to sing."[4] In that kind of singing we truly celebrate and keep feast. Aware that we have been made a people by God in order to journey to the kingdom, serving one another and our world, we sing out our praise at the marvel God has done and our neediness in the face of our unfinished journey and mission.

CATECHESIS FOR LITURGY

Attending. Liturgical catechesis begins with the task of attending to our experience of liturgical singing. What, we ask ourselves, do we actually experience when we sing?

If we wish to recover that experience by some form of reminiscing, one possibility is to have the group search our memories to surface the lasting associations we have all made between songs and different moments and experiences in our lives and relationships. Songs unlock a storehouse of memories of people, places, events, movies, and so on. Another possibility with a more explicitly liturgical focus is to have people recall a particular feast or season and then free-associate the songs which capture the feeling of the season for us in a deep and lasting way.

In the case of song, as with speech, it seems far more effective to recover the experience through some form of exercise. We might have the people close their eyes in reverie while the songs of a season are being played and relive whatever those songs evoke, as a way of discovering the power that songs have to sum up a season. Videotapes of familiar scenes, such as TV ads which use song, might be played with and without the sound track so that we experience the mutual impact and interplay of image and song. Or an excerpt of the recorded soundtrack from a familiar movie or broadway musical might be played to let us experience how the sound evokes the image and action it accompanied.

The best form of exercise, however, is a live experience of some kind. Our local director of music can easily put together a series of songs to help us experience the interaction of music and lyrics and the different ways in which song affects us. A variety of musical styles should be used; we might listen to some songs and sing others. An alternate approach is to invite a performing artist, such as a gospel singer, to sing for us and to lead us in song.

When we have recovered a sense of the experience, whether by reminiscing about or actually engaging in song, we are ready to begin describing what we have experienced. It is important to try to faithfully describe the actual experience and not move too quickly into interpretation. What aural features of the songs struck us? Was there anything about doing it together as a shared physical activity that caught our attention? What interplay did we sense between the music and the words? What did they do to each other?

To complete our task of recovering the experience, we need to name its inner quality. This should flow easily, given the capacity singing has to evoke and express inner feelings, memories, and associations. We are then ready to take up the second task.

Reflecting. The second task of liturgical catechesis is concerned with asking what that experience of liturgical singing means to us and to our community.

The first phase of this step is to gather up the impressions we have described and named above and begin to piece them together in larger wholes. The lead questions for us to discuss are questions of meaning. They should focus not only on the content of the lyrics, but also on the form and style of the song and the experience of singing it together. What does singing tell us about ourselves, about our mutual relations? What does it tell us about our world and our lives together in it? And above all, what does it tell us about our God and being God's people? What special feelings does it lend to all these? As we answer these questions, we always need to ask the further question: Why? What was there in the experience of the singing that evoked those feelings and ideas in us?

The second phase of this step is to explore the experience of our larger community with the help of resource people.

First, the scriptures have recorded the lyrics of many songs - the psalms of the Jewish people, and the hymns that dot the pages of the christian scriptures. Even though we can not learn much from the scriptures about the musical settings of these lyrics, a reflection on the texts themselves can be helpful, especially in view of the work now being done on a revision of the liturgical psalter.[5]

Second, we might invite the local music director to help us do a musical sampling from our people's history. A full history of liturgical music is less important than a sample which can help us understand the different ways in which we have matched music to text[6] and the different self-understandings our community has expressed in the various styles of music throughout our history.

Third, we might ask someone to highlight the more important perspectives and directives contained in the two documents the U.S. bishops have issued on liturgical music.[7]

Fourth, it could be enriching to invite people from minority cultures within our community or from another christian community to explore their traditions of liturgical singing with us.[8]

In each case, a concluding discussion to help us set our own experience in the context of what we have heard is called for.

Applying. The final task of liturgical catechesis is to ask ourselves how we can apply what we have learned to our future celebration of the liturgy.

The group should be encouraged to draw up our own resolutions, both individually and as a whole, as well as whatever recommendations we might wish to pass on to the liturgy committee for its work of preparing and evaluating music for our celebrations.

PREPARATION AND EVALUATION

Preparing liturgical music for our celebrations has undoubtedly been the largest single item on the agenda of liturgy committees since the renewal took effect. Sometimes it seems to be the only one. As we go about our task of preparing, song has more often than not been both the key to our success and the source of our frustration. There is much we can now learn from this backlog of experience.

In the chapter on preparation and evaluation we heard the recommendation that we distinguish between the actual task of preparing individual celebrations and the larger responsibilities for setting policies and an overall tone for those celebrations. In keeping with that recommendation, I would like to suggest that the liturgy committee's primary responsibility in the area of liturgical music is to help us keep our priorities straight as we go about the work of getting our celebrations ready. That is the context for the specific remarks which follow.

First, in our committee work we need to keep the pastoral goal of all liturgical celebration clearly focused. Full participation of the assembled people is our primary norm, in singing as in all other facets of the liturgy. The spiritual needs of the people and their capacity to participate in such a way that their needs are served is our final goal and guide.

Second, singing is an essential and privileged element of all celebration of the new liturgy. But it is not an isolated element; it is meant to serve, not to dominate (MCW #23). Our concern as a liturgy committee, then, will be for a liturgical style in which there is harmonious interplay of song and the entire set of liturgical languages, and for a style of liturgy in which song contributes to the proper rhythm and flow of the rite.[9]

Third, since song is such a pre-eminent way of enhancing the liturgy and heightening the participation of the assembly, we owe it to the assembly to secure trained, capable ministers of music and leaders of song, and to provide them with the necessary resources and continuing training.

Fourth, I suggest that the final and perhaps the most difficult thing for the liturgy committee to do is to clearly communicate to the musicians and those who prepare the actual celebrations the overall feeling we want a season or type of celebration to have, and then leave it to them. Directors of music also need to realize that communication is a two-way process.

Our recent experience has taught us that there are a number of potential problem areas we face in preparing our community's song. One of these is the difficulty of maintaining a healthy balance and creative tension between the artistic quality of our music and the pastoral needs and capabilities of our people. Another is our struggle to move away from a practice of "inserting of packets of song" to finding a way to give the liturgy an aura of musicality. In great measure we depend on what music is available and suited to our people. A problem related to what we said above about trained musicians and cantors is that of adequate budget. We are being made increasingly aware that paying just salaries for professional musicians and proper royalties for using and reproducing their works cannot be casually ignored in a church that would be just. And keeping music ministers and assembly supplied with good quality new materials as they appear can strain our best intentions as well as our budgets. A final problem lies hidden in our recent reliance on song as the best way, and often the only way, to enhance the liturgy and secure participation. The risk we run is that of overburdening our music and asking it to do more than it can. We need to attend much more to the whole range of liturgical languages we have been discussing in this book. These and similar problems appear regularly on our liturgy committee doorstep.

A wide variety of resources is available to help us in our sung prayer, and our music directors can help us fill out our committee book shelves.[10]

What qualities ought we look for as we prepare and evaluate liturgical singing for our celebrations? Many of the qualities presented in the chapter on qualities and criteria are particularly pertinent in regard to liturgical singing. To those we might add the following.

Norm: "Music should be considered a normal and ordinary part of any liturgical celebration" (LMT #13; MCW #23).

Prepare and evaluate:

1. *Song in service of rite.* "The structure of the liturgical unit will disclose the elements to be enhanced by music. ... The first place to look for guidance in the use and choice of music is the rite itself" (LMT #8). Evaluation question: Did song appropriately serve the structure and rhythmic flow of the rite?

2. *Form based on function.* The ministerial function of song is to intensify and enhance the words and actions of the rite. "The musical form employed must match its liturgical function" (LMT #11; also #7, 9–10). Did form match function?

3. *Progressive solemnity.* The general principle that music is to be a normal and ordinary part of any liturgical celebration "is to be interpreted in light of another one, namely, the principle of progressive solemnity. This later principle takes into account the abilities of the assembly, the relative importance of the individual rites and their constituent parts, and the relative festivity of the

liturgical day" (LMT #13). Did the singing in the celebration honor the principle of progressive solemnity?

4. *Pastoral quality.* Song for celebration must possess good artistic, liturgical, and pastoral quality. "The pastoral judgment ... must always be applied when choosing music. ... The music selected must express the prayer of those who celebrate, while at the same time guarding against the imposition of private meanings on public rites" (LMT #12; MCW #25-41). Did the song meet the pastoral criterion?

5. *Music ministry for full participation.* In good pastoral liturgy "the entire worshiping assembly exercises a ministry of music" with the help of members who possess special gifts "in leading the musical praise and thanksgiving" of the assembly (LMT #63; LMT #64-70; MCW #33-38). "The function of music is ministerial; it must serve and never dominate. Music should assist the assembled believers to express and share the gift of faith" (MCW #23). Did the music ministers enable the assembled worshipers to exercise their ministry of music?

Summary question: Did the assembled worshipers sing their praise and prayer in faith, joy, and unity?

Notes

1. Resources for this descriptive essay and for further reading are: Leonard Bernstein, *The Unanswered Question: Six Talks at Harvard* (Cambridge: Harvard University Press, 1976); Susanne K. Langer, *Philosophy in a New Key. A Study in the Symbolism of Reason, Rite, and Art* (Cambridge: Harvard University Press, 1969), 204-245; Edward Foley, *Music in Ritual: A Pre-Theological Investigation* (Washington, D.C.: The Pastoral Press, 1984); Joseph Gelineau, *The Liturgy Today and Tomorrow* (New York: Paulist Press, 1978), 82-94; Charles S. Pottie, *A More Profound Alleluia! Gelineau and Routley on Music in Christian Worship* (Washington, D.C.: The Pastoral Press, 1984).

2. "Tone painting," which strives for literal imitation, is the exception to this.

3. See Edward Foley, "Meaning, Musical Forms, and Faith," *Pastoral Music 7 #5* (June-July 1983) 11-15.

4. That is how a friend described the inner experience of Gospel singing in the black culture.

5. The International Commission on English in the Liturgy has published two sets of original translations and new musical settings for psalms used in the liturgy as part of a consultation project. A fine literary and musical commentary is included for each.

6. See, for example, Joseph Gelineau, "Music and Singing in the Liturgy," in Cheslyn Jones, Geoffrey Wainwright, and Edward Yarnold (ed.), *The Study of the Liturgy* (New York: Oxford University Press, 1978), 440–454, esp. 449–454.

7. Bishops' Committee on the Liturgy, *Music in Catholic Worship* (Washington, D.C.: USCC, 1972, revised 1983), and *Liturgical Music Today* (Washington, D.C.: USCC, 1982).

8. There are many rich resources around us: the songs which are so much a part of popular religious celebrations in the hispanic culture; the deep and powerful tradition of Gospel music in the black culture; the Christmas carols immigrants brought with them from Europe; the simple, *a cappella* hymnody of the Church of the Brethren; etc.

9. See, for example, the cadence charts given in John P. Mossi (ed.), *Modern Liturgy Handbook. A Study and Planning Guide for Worship* (New York: Paulist Press, 1976), 78–79.

10. In addition to the two documents from our bishops, *Music in Catholic Worship* and *Liturgical Music Today*, a committee might find it helpful to peruse: Lucien Deiss, *Spirit and Song of the New Liturgy* (Cincinnati: World Library Publications, 1976); Virgil C. Funk (ed.), *Music in Catholic Worship. The NPM Commentary* (Washington, D.C.: National Association of Pastoral Musicians, 1982); Dennis J. Geaney and Dolly Sokol, *Parish Celebrations. A Reflective Guide for Liturgy Planning* (Mystic, CT: Twenty-Third Publications, 1983), 48–56; Gabe Huck, *Liturgy with Style and Grace* (Chicago: Liturgy Training Program, 1984), 22–27; Gabe Huck and Virgil C. Funk (ed.), *Pastoral Music in Practice* (Chicago and Washington, D.C.: Liturgy Training Publications and National Association of Pastoral Musicians, 1981).

Epilogue

AT THE BEGINNING OF THIS BOOK I EXTENDED AN INVITATION
to think in larger ways about our common ministry of caring for
God's people at prayer. I invited you to attend to our people's
experience and to reflect on the many ways in which the liturgy
speaks to us. I thank you for accepting the invitation, and I now
extend a further invitation to use whatever in the book seems
good to you for your own ministry of catechesis and preparation
for the liturgy.